The Technique of Fashion Design

The Technique of Fashion Design

Brenda Naylor

B T Batsford Limited
London and Sydney

© Brenda Naylor 1975
ISBN 0 7134 3009 5
First published 1975

Filmset by Tradespools Ltd, Frome, Somerset
Printed in Great Britain by
The Anchor Press, Tiptree, Essex
for the publishers
B T Batsford Limited
4 Fitzhardinge Street
London W1H 0AH and
23 Cross Street, PO Box 586
Brookvale, NSW 2100, Australia

Contents

Acknowledgement

I am indebted to my editor Thelma M. Nye for her unflagging help, interest and advice throughout the writing of this book and without whose guidance I could not have attempted to cope with the intracacies of preparing the layout. My thanks are due to all who have given me their time and help. The photographs of manufacturing processes were supplied with assistance of 'British Clothing Manufacture'; the trimmings came from the John Lewis Partnership and give some idea of the wide variety available to the general public; examples of the work of outside process specialists were given me by S. Jacoby Ltd, J. Irwin Davis Ltd and Victomatic Trims. Mary Richardson gave me invaluable information and ideas for the section on using craftwork and decorative stitching. Maxwell Croft let me have photographs of garments in fur, John Beebe of the Leather Institute, Baily's of Glastonbury, Pierre Carron and Cherry Ltd, photographs of leather clothing; the International Wool Secretariat, the International Institute for Cotton, the Commission Européenne de Propagande pour la Soie and Courtaulds Ltd generously supplied me with photographs of their fibres as fashion fabrics.

London 1975   BN

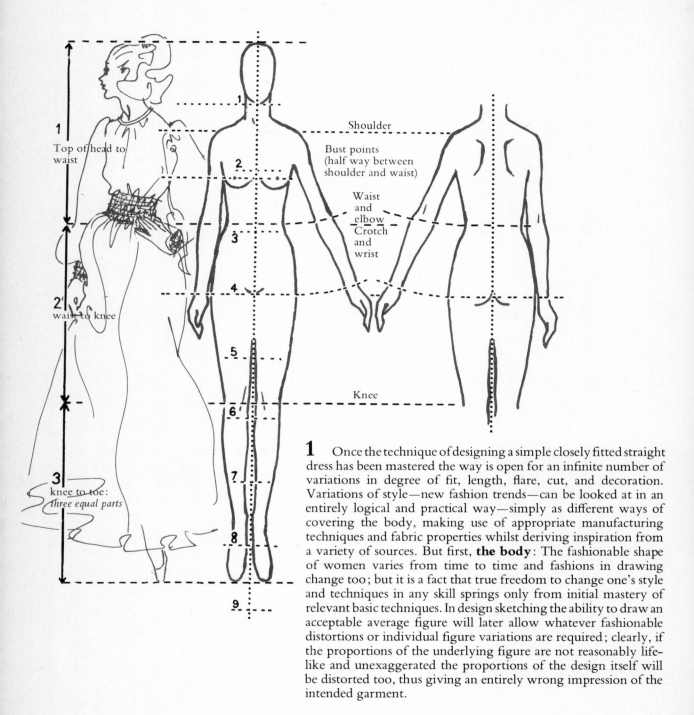

1 Top of head to waist

2 waist to knee

3 knee to toe: *three equal parts*

1

2

3

4

5

6

7

8

9

Shoulder

Bust points
(half way between
shoulder and waist)

Waist
and
elbow
Crotch
and
wrist

Knee

1 Once the technique of designing a simple closely fitted straight dress has been mastered the way is open for an infinite number of variations in degree of fit, length, flare, cut, and decoration. Variations of style—new fashion trends—can be looked at in an entirely logical and practical way—simply as different ways of covering the body, making use of appropriate manufacturing techniques and fabric properties whilst deriving inspiration from a variety of sources. But first, **the body**: The fashionable shape of women varies from time to time and fashions in drawing change too; but it is a fact that true freedom to change one's style and techniques in any skill springs only from initial mastery of relevant basic techniques. In design sketching the ability to draw an acceptable average figure will later allow whatever fashionable distortions or individual figure variations are required; clearly, if the proportions of the underlying figure are not reasonably life-like and unexaggerated the proportions of the design itself will be distorted too, thus giving an entirely wrong impression of the intended garment.

8

For each of the steps in the following design exercises draw (or trace) only as much of the basic figure as necessary. Most designers prefer to work with a layout pad and a B or 2B pencil or a ball-point pen; a good idea is to draw several figures of various sizes on a sheet of stiff paper which can then be slipped under layout paper and the designs drawn over them. Only the leg length has been slightly elongated in this basic figure, otherwise the proportions are standard.

2 Hold a piece of fabric against any part of the female figure and notice the folds that form from the prominent parts of the anatomy—the bust, shoulder blades, hip bones and buttocks. When this fullness is made into darts these almost invariably *end* in seams or edges. (The exceptions are those darts which go from bust point to bust point, from bust point to hip bone or from shoulder blade to buttock, but these are always combined with other darts or seams.) Fold a dart pointing out from the centre of any piece of paper and realize how essential it is to place—and draw—darts *only* from where the bumps in the anatomy occur. **The darts on the bodice front** start at the bust point. In theory, darts can be swung round in any direction so that they end in the waist, side, shoulder or centre-front seams, or at the neck edge or armhole, creating darts that are an attractive feature whilst still being entirely functional.

Not all women's garments have bust darts; clever cutting and manipulation of the fabric, stretch fabrics, flat-chested figures, foundations that result in smoother, less emphasized busts, certain fashion trends and different standards of fit render them, in some cases, unnecessary.

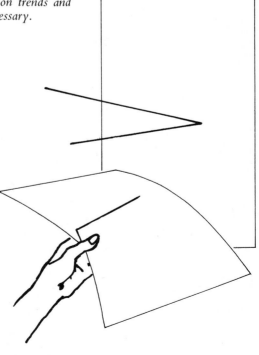

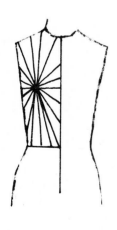

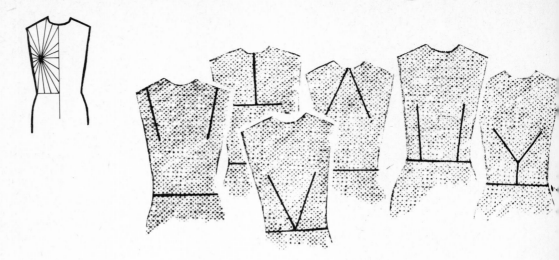

3 In practice **there are sometimes good reasons against dart manipulation**. It may be that the grain of the fabric, ie, the warp and the weft, is not firm enough and the darts would be unattractively distorted. In the case of fabric with a regular or clearly defined pattern it would be unwise to break it up in any but the least noticeable places; the same goes for checks, stripes and regular spots, unless a particularly noticeable and unusual effect is the aim and an experienced maker-up is to carry it out. As a rule when dealing with these patterns the area across the bodice from shoulders to bust and on down the centre front looks best smooth and unbroken.

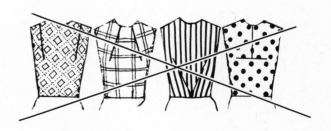

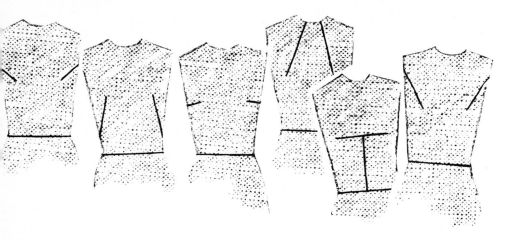

In fact, to allow for movement and because otherwise the effect would be rather ugly, darts start just short of the bust point—how short depends on the shape of the bust and the degree of fit required. Darts can be curved or have corners, but these *are* very eye-catching and they inevitably draw attention to the bust. Make sure they do not emphasize a bad bustline or create unfortunate effects.

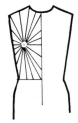

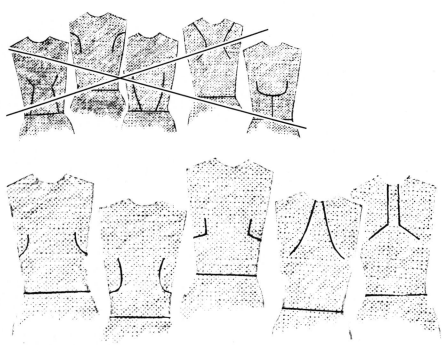

4 Depending on the individual figure—whether a gentler, more rounded shaping is to be preferred—or else to keep the warp as near vertical and the weft as near horizontal as possible, perhaps to help improve the over-all proportions—or simply for decorative effect, **more than one dart position may be employed.**

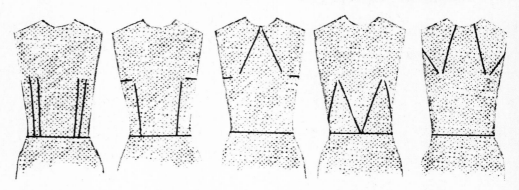

5 Perhaps with some of the previous examples, and certainly with darts such as these it is clearly more satisfactory from the point of view of making up, looks and facility of fitting to **extend the darts to meet in one smooth continuous line, cut as a seam** rather than darts but in every case, since these are closely-fitted garments, with the seams passing exactly over the bust points and, of course, starting and finishing in other seams—or edges.

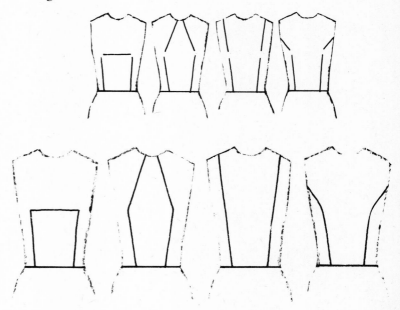

12

6 Hip darts start at the hip bones—usually flatter and less precisely situated parts of the anatomy than the bust points—therefore allowing for a little more flexibility in placing. They too can be swung and should be designed to complement the bodice seams or darts, either meeting them at the waist seam or repeating the angle.

7 The entire front may be shaped by seams—vertical, horizontal, diagonal—or mixed—to create attractive and totally functional effects, so long as they pass over the areas to be fitted—bust, waist and hips.

8 Skirts can be designed to flare by shaping the vertical panel or side seams as well as by more subtle addition or subtraction of fabric along horizontal and diagonal seams. In fact the whole art of pattern cutting really takes off from here . . .

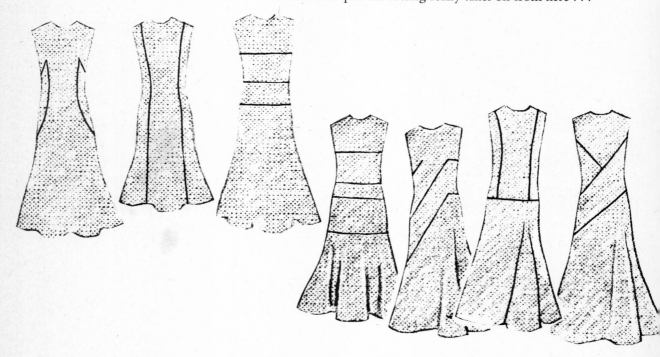

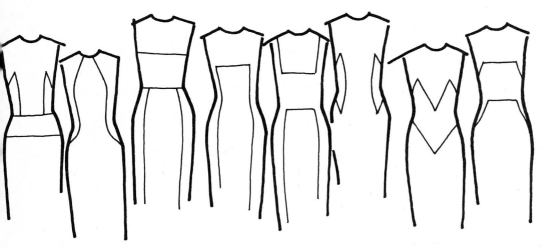

9 Darts and seams may combine:

10 **Construction lines can be curved at will** so long as they pass over the areas to be fitted *and are flattering*. Certain lines would be unflattering to most figures:

11   Interesting results can be achieved when, having performed their function of shaping, **construction lines continue for decorative purposes only** to form the focal point of the design.

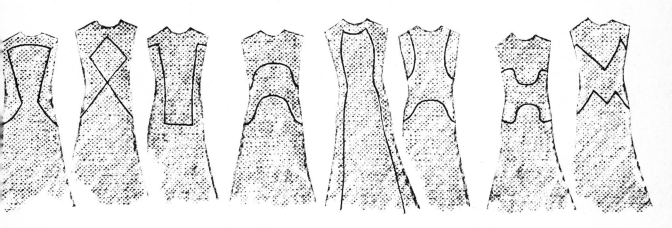

12   These effects can be made even more eye-catching by **contrasting or toning colours**, combinations of patterns and plains, differing textures or fabric types—*effects though to be used with caution.*

13 **Additional lines can be incorporated in a design.**
Seams may be emphasized by top-stitching, piping or decorative
braids; but these lines will be very noticeable indeed and the
designer needs to think very carefully about the effects created,
some of which make the wearer narrower and taller:

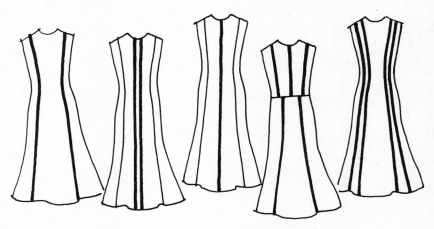

Some may make her appear wider and shorter:

14 **Diagonal lines** are the most concealing:

15 **A good asymmetric design can conceal a badly lop-sided figure:**

Lines may be used to widen one part of the figure and narrow another, conceal one section by drawing attention elsewhere:

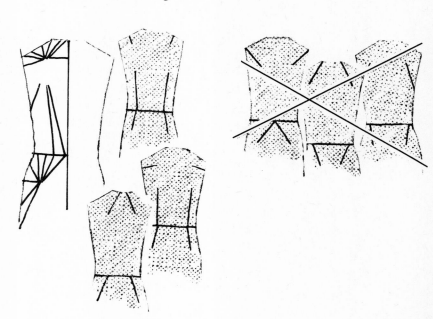

16   But **it is seldom a good idea to use a lot of tricks on one design**—better to start by selecting one seam or dart and then build up the rest of the design by using what seem to be the obvious complementary lines. Never *appear* to be trying too hard to be original; inevitably the design will end up looking contrived.

17   Just as with fronts, **backs of garments can be fitted by means of darts**. These can be swung at will from shoulder blades and hips, so long as grain and pattern will allow, to give an attractive and at the same time thoroughly practical result. Always try to flatter the figure; most women would not be very happy if their waist and hips were made to look larger than they actually are—and some lines at the back can give the appearance of round shoulders or a large seat.

18 **Backs may be shaped entirely or partly by seams:** and unless they are very short, closely-fitted straight dresses need some sort of allowance for movement designed into them—often in the back by means of pleats, splits, and wrap-overs.

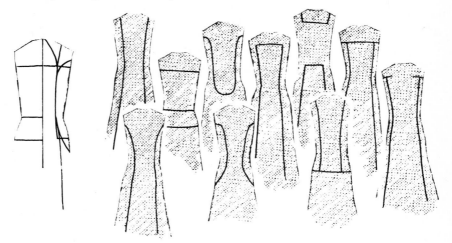

19 **Always make sure that any design features continue on round the body** and do not stop short at the side or shoulder seams.

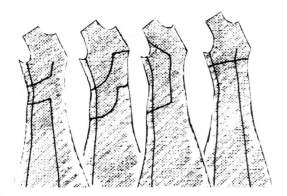

20 **If the neckline is not large enough for the head to pass through comfortably** provision has to be made for an opening. It may be that the centre back seam is a convenient place: manufacturers often insert a long zip from neck to hipline which makes for easy dressing as well as straightforward manufacture—and lazy design too, on occasions.

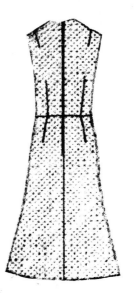

21　**Many garments today are styled so as not to need any fastenings at all**, often derived from peasant styles when presumably in the first place there were no fastenings available apart from a tie or drawstring of some sort. With specially designed leisure clothes which have no precise fitting the fewer fastenings the better and, so long as they are loose enough, it is perfectly possible to have semi-fitted or straight-hanging garments that need no fastenings, particularly if they are made in jersey or stretch fabrics.

22　Theoretically **cutting a garment on the bias** should give some sort of dimensional flexibility, clinging to the body and yet allowing free movement, as in some styles of the late twenties and early thirties. But this sort of bias cutting is usually avoided by manufacturers and home dressmakers alike, being fraught with difficulties; a skirt on the bias, even when hung for days to allow it to drop is likely to continue to drop long after the hem has been turned up and the garment is being worn (which perhaps explained the vogue for the uneven hemline). And where warp and weft are not precisely of equal weight and number of threads it is clearly impossible to get a predictably good outcome. Some bias cut in mass-production has been made possible by the use of bonded fabrics, a process which entails two fabrics, one of them usually an acetate lining, being stuck together, which makes the dimension and behaviour of the fabric entirely predictable. Fusible interlinings enable sections of garments to be cut on the bias for decorative effect, but notice how much narrower these sections look when checks or stripes are used; so avoid using them anywhere on designs where a slimming effect is not a good thing; for example, if the shoulders are made to look narrower the rest of the body automatically looks wider as a result.

23 Very closely-fitted dresses necessarily need rather rigid foundation garments but **modern fashions in underwear—as well as the fashion for no underwear—allow top clothes that do not have such a precise fit.** Semi-fitted, seamed dresses allow for more figure variation and easy movement than tight, darted ones and when made in jersey fabrics are even better. It *is* possible to steam-press some woollen fabrics to shape but this is rarely satisfactory for a woman with any but a small bust. We hear about moulded dresses from time to time but the very process of permanently shaping any substance so that it would adequately fit the complex shape of the average woman's body means that they could not possibly have the suppleness and flexibility to adapt themselves gracefully to figure variations and the movement of the body and therefore could only be considered for crisp, semi-fitted styles or unfitted garments.

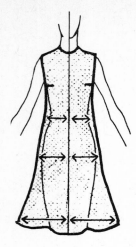

24 **Semi-fitted clothes** are sketched over the same basic figure. Gravity and the weight of the fabric will ensure that they lie along the original shoulder line, standing away from the figure from the bustline downwards. Always check that the measurements out from the centre line at waist, hips and hem are equal on both sides to ensure that a sketch is symmetrical. The less closely fitted the garment, the less the need to shape the fabric—or draw the shaping—exactly to the contours of the body as previously described; darts and seams can be moved around a little to give a better over-all look and, greatly to the advantage of the mass-manufacturer, fit a far larger number of figure variations within the size-range. For example, a raised waistline with a slightly flared skirt will eliminate the need for accurate individual waist and hip fitting.

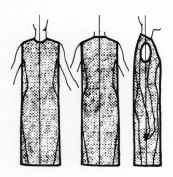

25 **Straight garments** hang—and are drawn—straight down from the shoulders or bustline:

26 **Flared garments** can flare from the shoulders—or lower down. This will naturally depend upon the cut, but when sketching a flared or full garment, unless there is to be specific fullness at one point, the silhouette (which includes the hemline) indicates the degree of fullness—which will naturally be distributed all round the figure.

27 The fashionable silhouette has undergone many changes in recent years. A woman's appearance and proportions can be altered almost out of recognition by variations in the height of the waistline and hem, style of sleeve, the bulk and amount of fabric used, the degree of fit, shape of the shoulders, as well as her hairstyle, hats, jewelry, shoes, stockings, colouring, make-up— even the way she stands and moves. Luck, timing, publicity, finance . . . all play their part in a new fashion being accepted by the general public, some trends taking longer than others to become established, others being little more than of passing interest. The dates give an approximate guide.

ost 1918— Early twenties———Mid twenties ————— Early thirties ———— Mid thirties—

—Late thirties ———————— Wartime 1939–45 ———— Postwar —New Look ——————— Early fifties—

Mid fifties — Late fifties — Early sixties —

Mid sixties — Late sixties — Early seventies —

26

28   In these days when a woman can wear almost anything, or nothing, and not appear out of place it is still a fact that very low necklines only look really right on the beach, in the evening, at home—or on pinafore dresses. **A plain round neckline can be of any height**, and it can provide a good starting point for a design. To take the two extremes:

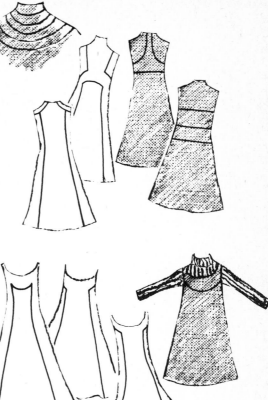

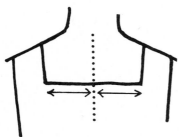

29   **A neckline can be cut to any shape** and faced, bound or trimmed. When sketching necklines from a direct front view, just as when actually cutting them to a shape, both sides must measure the same.

30 Manufacturers sometimes **use trimmings to finish edges decoratively**, usually at the same time dispensing with the need for facings. The same techniques can be used for any other edge —hemlines, armholes or sleeve edges.

31 In these designs based on high and low necklines the waistline is sometimes in the natural place, sometimes higher or lower, but always a single straight line. **Waistlines can also be shaped or curved or emphasized** in some way: and obviously they need not necessarily be only on closely-fitted clothes.

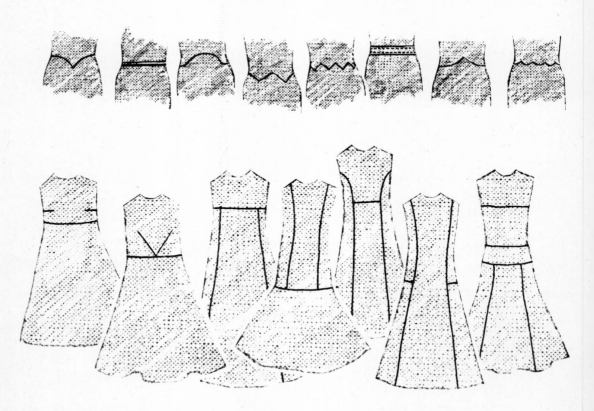

32 **Hemlines**, dictated to a certain extent by fashion, can be of any height and, being also a cut edge, can be shaped, trimmed, emphasized or decorated at will.

33 **Armholes** can be designed to take a set-in sleeve or to remain sleeveless—faced, bound or trimmed. Undergarments must stay out of sight so the armholes of sleeveless dresses are often cut slightly higher under the arms than those with sleeves. In either case when viewed from the front or back they appear, and are sketched, as a straight line. Always bearing in mind that the undergarments must not show armholes can be cut to any decorative shape and, trimmed or not, make an interesting design feature.

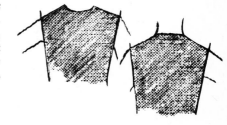

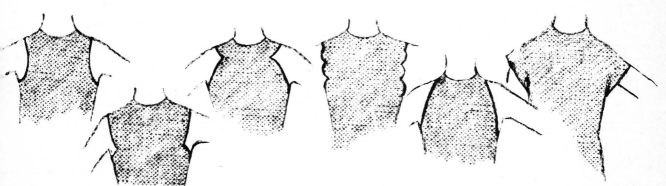

34 There are differences of opinion as to the names of some **sleeves and armholes**. In any case so many variations on the basic cuts are possible that it is just not practicable to try to give each one a precise name. For instance, these are all variations on the classic raglan:

Here are some other styles:

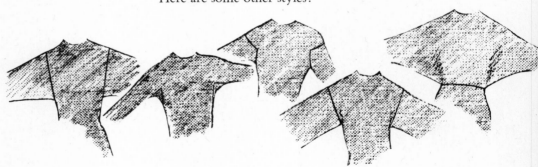

The sleeves can vary too, in length:

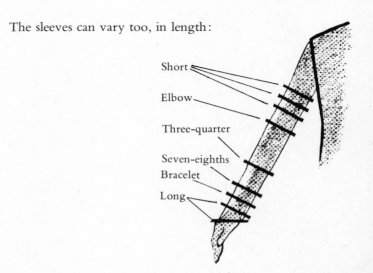

30

width:

shape and size of cuff:

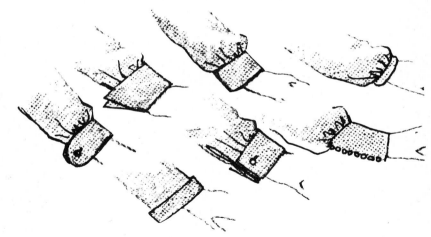

and style:

35   When a designer tries too hard to be original the result is almost inevitably a contrived and unnatural-looking article. As in all things to be *seen* to be trying too hard is a mistake; the most satisfactory end-products are always those which appear to have materialized quite naturally and without the slightest effort on the part of the designer—and in dress these are always garments that are related to the body underneath and are flattering and helpful to any woman's figure and proportions, which allow for easy and graceful movement and which do not have conflicting or too numerous points of interest. **A good way to begin a design** is to start off with one clear feature. Start, for example, with a neckline: Then sketch in the *facts* of the design as dictated by fashion, fabric, the type of garment wanted and any other relevant facts—in this case just the appropriately fashionable silhouette and suitable hemline. Turn back to the dart and seam shaping diagrams and select a line that complements the neckline. *Go for the obvious first* and it may well turn out to be the most satisfactory in the end.

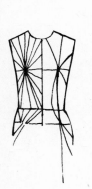
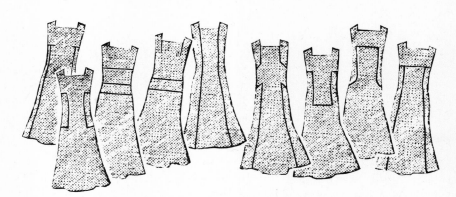

In contrast, here are some examples of lines that do not complement the neckline:

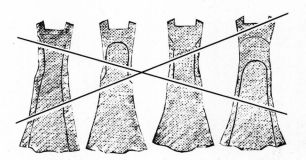

Here is a differently shaped neckline, again showing some lines that complement the neckline and some that do not:

36 When the neckline, construction and silhouette *are* in harmony, how easy it is then to **emphasize features of the design** by using tricks, two fabrics, colours or textures, adding simple sleeves if appropriate and then designing the backs by simply continuing the lines in a flattering manner and making sure that there is both access and ease of movement.

37 **Godets, pleats and gathers are ways of putting movement into a skirt** and are often the main feature of a design. They do need to be sketched with great care and accuracy so that neither maker-up nor client can misinterpret the designer's intention. Godets are triangular pieces of fabric inserted into a seam or split that will give localized fullness at the hem, both in the garment itself and in the sketch. Godets can be wide or narrow, plain or pleated:

38 **Pleats** in a sketch have a definite beginning and end. Even in the case of a sunray pleated skirt—which is made from two quarter-circles of fabric, the pleating carried out by professional pleaters—the lines start from the hipline and go on down, unbroken, to the hemline. As with all pleats it is only by the accurate drawing of the hemline that anyone can tell with certainty which type of pleat is intended. Crystal pleating, again done by professional pleaters, is on the straight of the fabric so that the lines on the sketch will start precisely at the waist seam or yoke. As before, each line will continue unbroken down to the hem.

39 **Other types of pleats can be made by the maker-up.** A heavier weight of line indicates that pleat and not seam is intended, or show the point at which seam becomes pleat. Pleats can be decorated, emphasized, held in place, by stitching. The drawing of the hemline is all-important.

40 **Unpressed pleats** are unmistakably indicated by the drawing of hem and silhouette. In the second sketch the silhouette shows without a shadow of doubt that the skirt is fitted over the hips by means of seams which then flare out quite sharply; all turnings are pressed in one direction and the hem turned up before

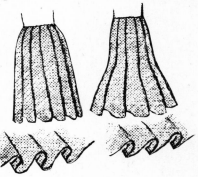

the hem is finally stitched. Unpressed pleats are an alternative method of fitting to the use of darts or seams, useful because they allow for some figure variation or a range of differently shaped foundation garments. Sometimes darts are only stitched part-way, then left as unpressed pleats.

41   **Gathers** are one of the simplest methods of varying a design. They can be used in a number of places on a garment, but use them with care because they do add bulk. In every case the type and design of the fabric should be taken into account. Gathers would be quite unsuitable, for example, in a plaid, thick tweed, leather, fur fabric or vinyl. Provided that a few basic rules are borne in mind they are easy to sketch. The first rule is that they must start from a seam-line, *not* just above or below it. The lines are of varying lengths, some of them extending right to the hem. The drawing of the edge itself, and of the silhouette, will indicate the amount of fullness in the frill; clearly, a lot of fullness drawn at the top of the frill and very little at the hem and silhouette would be quite wrong.

42   Strips of any width can be gathered into **frills** which can then be used to give a variety of effects.

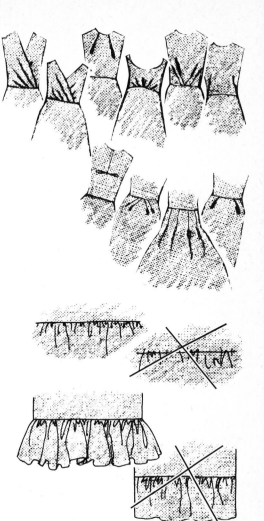

The strips can be gathered down the middle instead of along one edge.

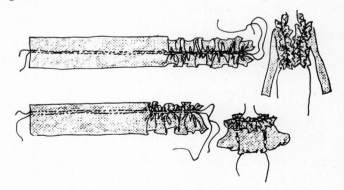

Complete sections of garments can be gathered.

As always, the rest of the design should complement the detail rather than ignore, conflict or distract from it.

43 **Flounces** are strips of any width cut from the circumference of a circle; the smaller the circle, the greater the fullness. When the shorter edge is joined to a straight edge—or to a neckline—the strip falls into deepening folds. For extra fullness flounces may be gathered.

44 The method of cutting a flounce is basically the same as that for cutting **circular and half-circular skirts**. Notice that when sketching this type of skirt the lines of the folds never quite reach the waist or yoke seam, except where the waistline is cut purposely larger with the intention of gathering it to give extra fullness. Notice how the hems are drawn.

45 **Gathering is yet another method of shaping the fabric to the figure** in a decorative manner, swinging the fullness around just as in dart manipulation and swathing the fabric closely to the body (and not necessarily symmetrically).

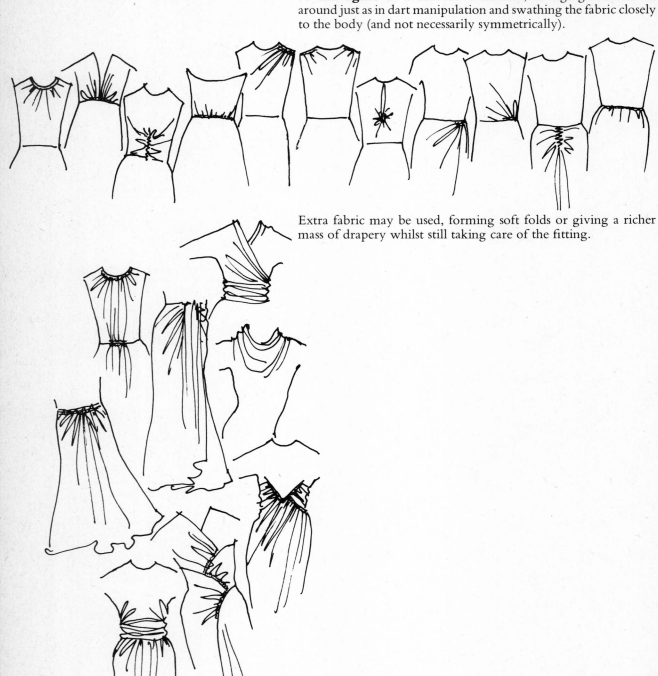

Extra fabric may be used, forming soft folds or giving a richer mass of drapery whilst still taking care of the fitting.

Yokes as well as seams are good starting points for gathers, drapery and folds.

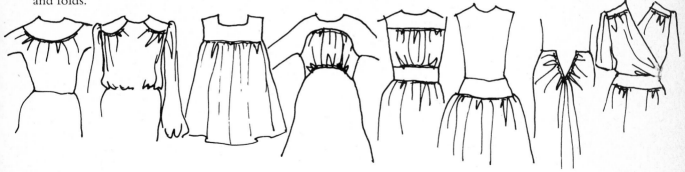

46   Elastic used in a design featuring gathers (or, alternatively, designs incorporating *sections* of stretch fabric) can dispense entirely with the need for fastenings—and this should always be the case in **shirred garments**, with the possible exception of designs with a high neckline.

39

47 **Belts** can be used to control gathers and can in any case be important design features, be they plain or fancy, wide or narrow, matching or contrasting. The belt carriers themselves can be part of the design, or as inconspicuous as possible.

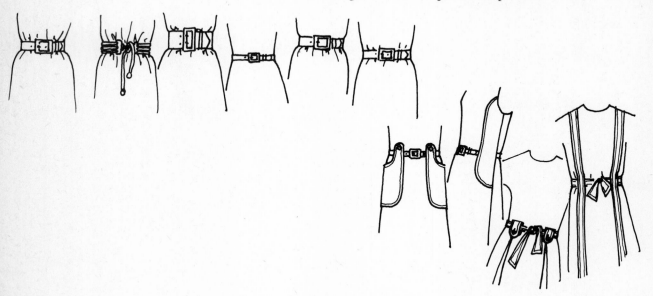

48 **Elasticated waistlines** (or elastic in a channel) are particularly useful in casual skirts, trousers or leisure garments or in clothing for some handicapped people who have limited movement or hand function or difficulty in using other types of fastenings.

49   How to get in and out of clothes must always be borne in mind, as mentioned earlier; many fastenings and openings can be more than purely functional. It is only comparatively recently that designers have used **zip fasteners as decorative features**. Some today are made in large scale although still light in weight; many are attractively coloured and/or combined with fancy braids, intended to be stitched to the outside of an opening rather than underneath it—a useful technique when designing for quickly made casual garments in leather or non-fray fabrics. Zips for coats and jackets are open-ended. Zip openings are simple to design (any garment that has or could have a centre front seam can have a zip there) and cut; they need little planning, no wrap, and virtually no extra fabric beyond the normal seam allowances. Zip sliders can have rings or fancy tabs, or a pull can be made from a strip or rouleau of the garment fabric or any other suitable material, easy to manipulate and at the same time an attractive design feature. Set into easy-to-reach seams—the centre-front, shoulder or raglan seams for instance—zips can become the focal point of a design, and incidentally be a real boon to people who have difficulty in dressing.

50   **Velcro, the touch-and-close fastener**, can also be useful in some circumstances. It is not as satisfactory used in long strips as in small 'dabs' which are much easier to place together accurately (and *Velcro has* to be placed together accurately or the entire garment will be distorted) and which will avoid the 'bow-fronted' look that inevitably occurs when an individual sits down and relaxes in any garment which has a rather rigid continuous fastening down the front.

51   Haberdashery departments stock **a wide variety of fastenings**—hooks and eyes, poppers, press studs, eyelets . . . that make useful alternatives to the more conventional methods.

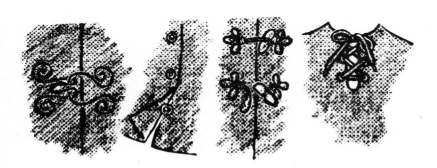

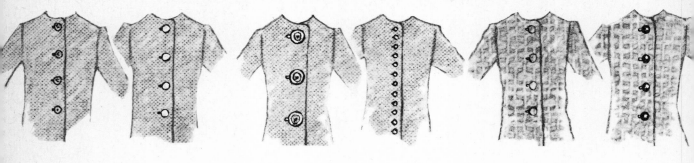

52 **Buttons** can affect the over-all look of a design to such an extent that their effect needs to be considered very carefully. Matching or contrasting, large or small, discreetly covered or as eye-catching as possible, my personal view is that they should never be placed anywhere where they do not either perform, or appear to perform, their correct function—that of holding two sections of a garment together. (I have only once seen buttons used purely decoratively to good effect and that was where large pearl buttons were stitched closely together on the collar and cuffs of a dress in place of embroidery).

53 **Buttons need to be sketched with care**, of identical size, correctly spaced and with buttonholes of appropriate size—as the sketches show.

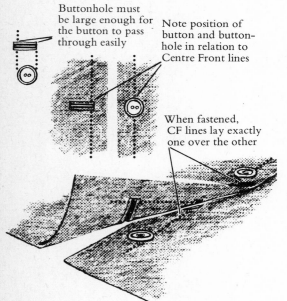

Buttonhole must be large enough for the button to pass through easily

Note position of button and buttonhole in relation to Centre Front lines

When fastened, CF lines lay exactly one over the other

54 **The buttoned placket found mostly on tee-shirts** and sports shirts consists of strips of fabric positioned to hide the raw edges of a slit and stitched. The turnings of a seam can be extended to form a placket, in which case the drawing needs to be particularly precise so that there is no mistaking what the designer intends by way of seam and opening.

55 **The buttons on a single-breasted garment** are always situated exactly down the centre, never touching the edge of the wrap-over which is to one side or the other of the centre—depending on whether it is a man's or a woman's garment. (In all cases the two sides of the garment are identical.) It may be helpful at first to pencil in all the construction lines, shown here as dotted lines, until the correct placing becomes automatic. The drawing can be done with a ball or fibre point pen and the construction lines erased; alternatively if lay-out paper is being used construction lines can be pencilled in for guidance on the *reverse* side of the paper.

56 For **double-breasted garments** the same rules apply except that here the buttons are situated equally to either side of the centre line, only those down the side nearest the wrap-over edge having buttonholes. Note that with most double-breasted garments there should be some relation between the silhouette, the placing of buttons and the shape of the wrap-over edge.

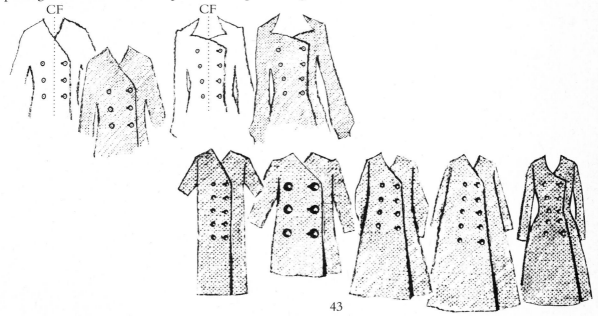

43

57 When **sketching coats and jackets** draw the edge of the wrap-over and the hemline of that side as one continuous line and the hemline of the other side either not quite touching it or seeming to go behind it, as the sketches show. Thickening of the line or a little shading can help to give the right effect, which it must not be possible to confuse with that of a seam. Never sketch the silhouette of a jacket over skirt or trousers as a continuous line; it must show that it lies over them, however closely-fitted the style or thin the fabric. Thick fabrics and less closely-fitted jackets naturally stand away more.

58 Women with less-than-perfect necks do not look their best in clothes with starkly simple necklines. A collar—by definition an extension of the garment that, as a rule, turns back over on itself can do much to flatter or hide this feature that is one of the first to show signs of age—and also do much to keep it warm. It is important that a collar is in scale with the rest of the garment, not too big or too small for the individual or for current fashion proportions—important too that it does not engulf a short neck or expose an exceptionally long one. Some collars lay flat, others are built up, some stand up and some stand away; they can be of any size. The cut edge can be shaped, and the collar itself decorated, trimmed, emphasized and made in self fabric or material of contrasting colour or texture. **The classic tailored collar** is one of the most versatile styles. Those who, at first, find it difficult to draw correctly will find it helpful to remember that *both sides of the collar are identical.* Follow the drawings step by step, pencilling in the construction lines until no longer necessary.

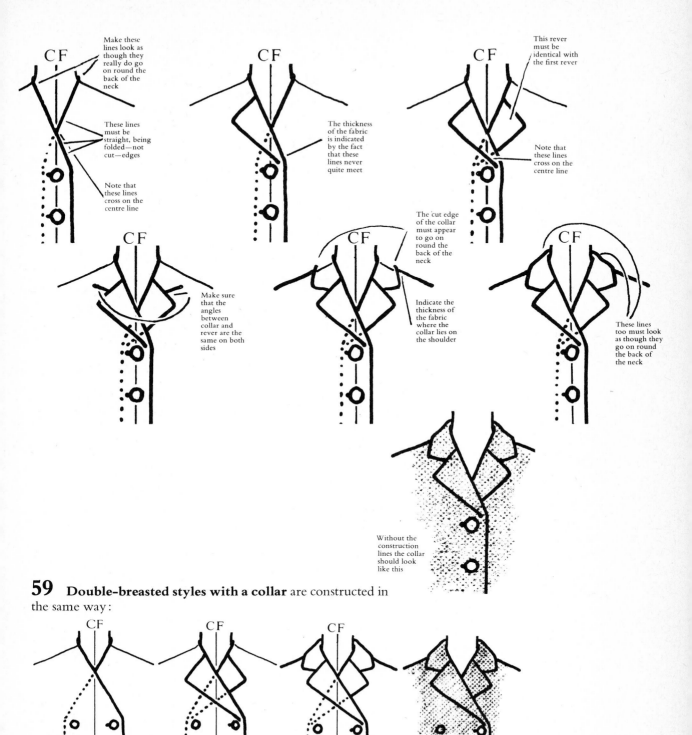

Make these lines look as though they really do go on round the back of the neck

CF

These lines must be straight, being folded—not cut—edges

Note that these lines cross on the centre line

CF

The thickness of the fabric is indicated by the fact that these lines never quite meet

CF

This rever must be identical with the first rever

Note that these lines cross on the centre line

CF

Make sure that the angles between collar and rever are the same on both sides

CF

The cut edge of the collar must appear to go on round the back of the neck

Indicate the thickness of the fabric where the collar lies on the shoulder

CF

These lines too must look as though they go on round the back of the neck

Without the construction lines the collar should look like this

59 Double-breasted styles with a collar are constructed in the same way:

CF   CF   CF

45

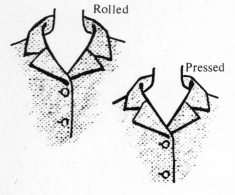

Rolled

Pressed

60 **When a collar stands away from the neck** this may be indicated by the use of a little shadow and by the way that the *fold* lines are not drawn close to the base of the neck. Whether the collar rolls over gradually or is crisply pressed is shown by the silhouette and by the fact that the fold line is curved, as well as by the nearness of the fold to the outline.

61 Notice the points where **the drawing of a collar in thick fabric** differs from one in thin fabric:

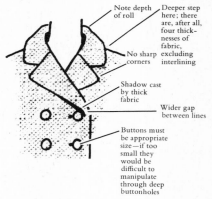

Note depth of roll

Deeper step here; there are, after all, four thicknesses of fabric, excluding interlining

No sharp corners

Shadow cast by thick fabric

Wider gap between lines

Buttons must be appropriate size—if too small they would be difficult to manipulate through deep buttonholes

62 **Variations of the classic tailored collar** are suitable for a wide range of garments:

63 Here are **more collars**, starting with the adaptable shirt collar with a stand that can be worn open or closed, with shaped or buttoned-down points, stitched or plain . . .

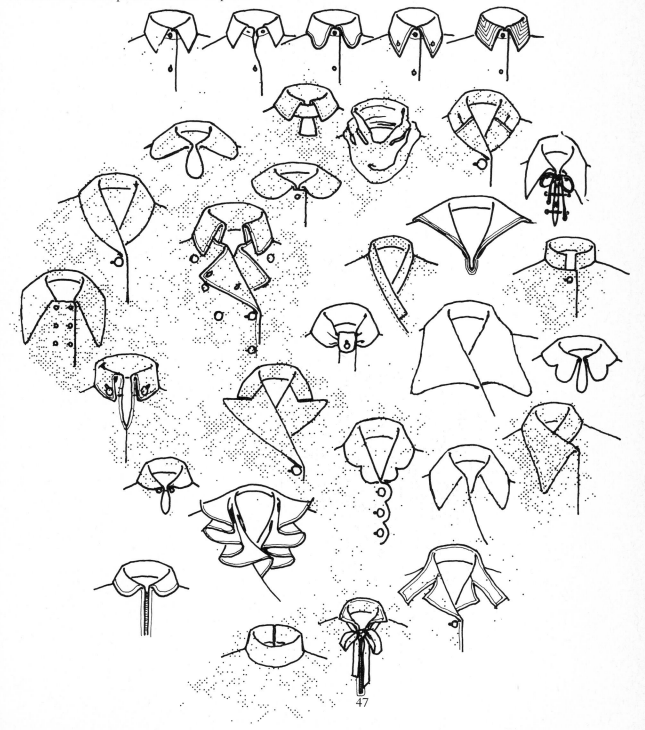

47

64 **Patch pockets,** usually—but not necessarily—made from the same fabric as the rest of the garment, are extremely simple to make and yet can be an important addition to any design. Thoughtfully positioned on bodice, skirt or even sleeve they can be both useful and decorative. Easy access and the likely contents are the practical points to remember; from the point of view of the over-all appearance badly placed pockets can make hips look wider, busts lower, or they can look totally out of scale with the rest of the garment. Well placed pockets can attract attention and make the simplest dress look interesting.

Patch pockets can be of any suitable size or shape, but any decoration or trimming should tie in with that on the rest of the garment. Once on the body a garment becomes rounded; therefore, so as not to distort the way it hangs, patch pockets obviously ought not to be pinned in place whilst it is flat.

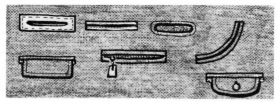

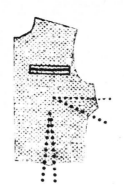

65 **Bound pockets**, contrasting or matching, straight or curved, sometimes incorporating zips or flaps, are best completed whilst the work *is* flat and before all the garment sections are put together. Never place them where they cannot be easily reached or where the contents will create unwanted bulges. Try to utilize the hollows of the body so that the silhouette will be affected as little as possible (remembering that the contents will settle at the *bottom* of the pockets). Watch that things will not pop out when the wearer bends over or sits down.

66 **Pockets in seams**, again bearing in mind easy access and the need not to create bulk, are planned before the garment is cut out because they are usually extensions of seam turnings. Top-stitching can decorate as well as fix the pocket in place.

49

67 **Most garments need pockets** of one sort or another; they are essential on winter coats for hands or gloves, indispensable on all outer garments for tickets, handy cash, sunglasses, etc when travelling and wonderfully useful on working clothes—waistcoats or aprons, for example . . .

68 Although in the past worn occasionally, and mainly for purely practical reasons, since 1966/7 and the introduction of trouser *suits*, **trousers** have become a staple ingredient of nearly every woman's wardrobe. At first often of a cut that left much to be desired and usually worn with jackets that had obviously been styled by designers more accustomed to cutting jackets to be worn over skirts, trousers for women now are no longer simply the equivalent of the masculine counterpart but an established feminine garment—as firmly established as coats, skirts, dresses, blouses and jackets and subject, as they are, to the fluctuations of fashion. Trousers come in a wide variety of cuts and fabrics, some of them for purely practical wear and others as feminine as long skirts. Most are cut appreciably longer these days, intended to be worn with truly feminine high-heeled shoes. A basic trouser shape is easy to draw and the sketches show how any variations can be sketched from that.

51

69   In order to produce satisfactory, workable designs for mass
production it is essential to know something of **the methods of
the clothing manufacturer**, the man with the showroom, the
sales organization and, usually, the brand name. Either he manu-
factures all his own garments or else he sub-contracts all or part
of his production to individual master tailors or outside contract
workers. A clothing factory will be laid out with the aim of
producing, economically, a certain number of a particular type of
garment compatible with the machinery and skilled labour on
hand. Naturally the lay-out will have some flexibility so as to cope
with fashion and circumstances, and new machinery will need to
be acquired from time to time.

Even in a fully mechanized factory there are a few processes that
cannot be done by machine—such as the finishing and felling of
linings, the finishing of the insides of piped buttonholes, the
sewing-on of fabric-covered or fancy buttons, hand pressing and
any stitching that cannot be done by blind stitching machine;
this might be the attaching of a hook and eye at the neckline or the
sewing on of some detail, perhaps a bow or a flower. The making
of details such as tabs, bows and scallops also requires some hand-
work. Something like fringing, as opposed to using fringe
trimming, might be sent out to individuals known to the firm.

70   **The manufacturer often uses fancy trimmings**, simpli-
fying and cutting down on the making up processes and decorating
the garments at the same time. Flexibility, washability and suppleness must be compatible with the fabric being trimmed.

52

Trimmings

1 5 cm long hair coney fur trimming
2 Smocked nylon filling
3 Slotted nylon filling
4 Nylon lace
5 5 cm nylon fur-fabric trimming
6 Tortion lace
7 Russia braid
8 Fancy button
9 Fold–over braid
10 Fancy button
11 Metallic fringe
12 Cotton carpet fringe
13 Guipure motif
14 Plaited braid
15 Nylon satin ribbon
16 Giant rick-rack
17 Cotton swiss braid
18 Nylon filling
19 Ostrich and maribou
20 Cotton faggoting
21 Cotton swiss braid
22 Pearl and metallic braid
23 Nylon edging
24 Fancy button
25 Metallic braid
26 Fancy button
27 Military braid
28 Rick-rack
29 Cluny lace
30 Greek key-pattern braid
31 Nylon lace
32 Narrow nylon lace edging
33 Guipure motif trimming
34 Single sequin trimming
35 Maribou trimming

71   Sometimes fabric will be sent to **outside process specialists** who have a variety of complicated and expensive machines and employ highly skilled operators to process customers' own materials in a variety of ways before being returned for incorporation into garments. Frequently pre-cut garment sections are worked on by individual operators who apply fancy braids and cords in intricate patterns, often combined with nailhead and rhinestone embroidery. All-over sequin embroidery is stitched onto fabric in patterns. Fine permanent pleating, plain or fancy, is done by machine. Versatile multi-needle machines will produce a variety of tucks or can, for instance, combine blade tucks and fancy stitching whilst at the same time decorating those tucks with loop edges or applying rows of lace. Ornate smocking, gauged or flat, is produced just as quickly as the material can pass through the machine. The same goes for rows of chain stitching, faggoting and saddle stitching. A strip of plain fabric fed into another machine comes out as rouching; up to nine rows of lace can be rouched onto a flat piece of fabric at one time. Quilting is done by the yard in a variety of designs. Narrow bias-cut strips of fabric are transformed into rouleaus, stitched and turned at the same time by yet another machine. As well as carrying out expressed wishes of his customers, the outside process specialist is constantly thinking up new ideas, new ways of using his machinery to stimulate their interest and sometimes provide inspiration for their designs.

The work of the outside process specialist

1 Saddle stitching
2 Gauged smocking, picot edging
3 Rouleau lattice
4 Cording
5 Rouched bands with flat lace
6 Pin tucks
7 Cording with drawn-thread work
8 Cornelly embroidery with metallic yarn
9 Reverse of saddle stitching with stud embroidery
10 Quilting
11 Blade tucks
12 Flat smocking
13 Elasticated smocking with metallic yarn
14 Cord embroidery with metallic yarn, combined with studs and metallic motifs
15 Flat smocking with metallic motifs
16 Open-ended crystal pleating
17 String cornelly embroidery with stud embroidery
18 Guipure lace motifs applied with studs
19 Elasticized gauging, using lace
20 All-over sequin embroidery
21 Braid embroidery
22 Fancy quilting
23 Fancy pleating, simulating rouching
24 Elasticated gauged smocking
25 Fancy pinch pleating, using studs
26 Fancy cord embroidery
27 Faggoting
28 Cornelly cording embroidery with stud embroidery
29 Fine permanent flat embroidery
30 Motif-drawing with cornelly machine
31 Rick-rack and braid embroidery
32 Rick-rack, cornelly machine-applied braid, guipure motifs with studs
33 Fancy crystal pleating
34 Lace-edged frills applied with faggoting
35 Braid, simulating stripes
36 Flat smocking with guipure braid
37 Quilting
38 Fancy flat pleating, vandyke effect
39 Pinch tucking and cording
40 Braid embroidery using metallic thread, stud and diamanté embroidery

72 Other specialists turn fabrics into buttons and belts.

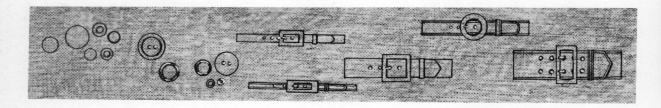

73 All of the trimmings illustrated, as well as the simple pleating, belt and button-making services, are available to the individual maker-up and manufacturer alike—not so the services of the outside process specialist. But with the newly awakened interest in needlecrafts of all kinds a far wider range of possibilities exists for really **unusual and individual garment decoration**. A few of those possibilities are illustrated here, ideas both simple and complicated; but the decoration should never look like an afterthought applied to a finished garment; rather it should be an integral part of the original design, to be worked out beforehand and incorporated into the garment at the appropriate moment during making up in the same way that a manufacturer would plan the making up of a mass-produced garment. As a result the finished garment will look elegant and fashionable, and not in the least homespun.

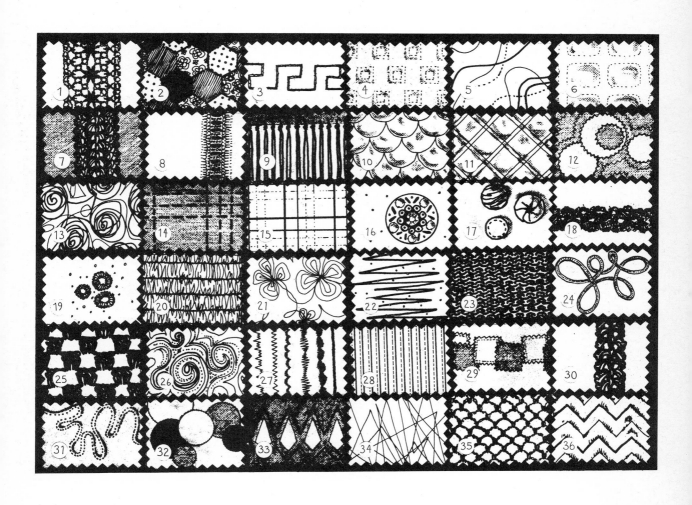

Craftwork and detail, individually done by hand and machine

1 Bobbin lace
2 Patchwork
3 Couching
4 Trapunto quilting
5 All-over free machine stitching, using different threads and stitches
6 Trapunto quilting
7 Machine-knitted braid, pressed open
8 Bead and thread hand embroidery
9 Fringing and blanket stitch
10 English quilting
11 English quilting on wool fabric, with knitting trim
12 Fabric collage applied and decorated with zigzag machine stitching
13 All-over free motif machine-stitching, using different threads
14 Pattern darning
15 Machine stitching with different threads to simulate plaid
16 Bead and diamanté embroidered covered buttons and surrounding area
17 Leather-covered buttons
18 Crocheted braid with multi-coloured bouclé wool
19 Shisha work
20 Shirring
21 Free machine drawing
22 Haphazard machine-stitching with metallic thread, bead embroidery by hand
23 Knitting—hand or machine
24 Braid embroidery, hand stitched with metallic thread
25 Crochet
26 Re-embroidered print
27 Machine embroidery, various stitches
28 Tucking by hand
29 Pinked, hand-stitched leather collage
30 Machine-knitted braid
31 Italian quilting
32 Collage, hand stitched
33 Hand-stitched padded appliqué and couching
34 Haphazard machine stitching
35 Irish crochet
36 Padded and flat quilting with two different threads

63

74 It pays the dressmaker to study the methods of the mass-manufacturer. Recent developments—**the use of fusible interlining and fabric bonding** for example—have made his work simpler. A range of fusible interlinings is available to all and, whilst individuals cannot have their own fabrics bonded, many useful combinations of fabrics are obtainable in the stores. The use of bonded fabrics has already been referred to in the section on bias cutting; clearly if the behaviour of fabric during manufacture and wear is entirely predictable this is all to the good. The widely used bonded lining of acetate locknit feels pleasant next to the skin, makes normally impractical fabrics suitable for use in mass-production by eliminating fraying and distortion during the making up and also does away with the need for additional lining. (Many manufacturers nevertheless choose to bind raw edges for a really good-looking finish.)

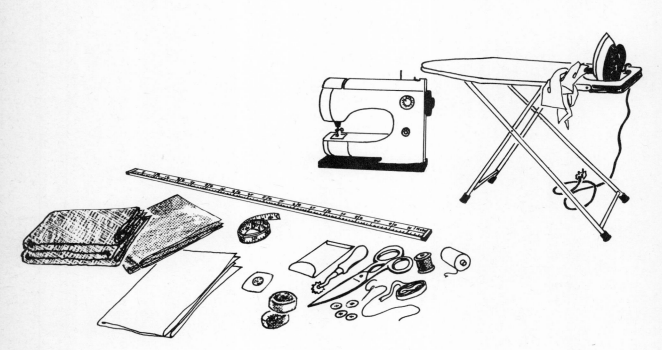

75 The way the work is planned in a factory, specializing in this first instance in manufacturing tailored suits, is entirely logical and has many **useful pointers for the home dressmaker** who, similarly, should ensure that everything that will be needed is to hand and trimmings, interlinings and linings bought; if there is to be any treatment of the fabric to entire sections of the garment this must have been done in advance. Fabric must have been shrunk or pressed if necessary, and all cutting and sewing equipment gathered together.

76 First **the manufacturer prepares his lay**; this involves the planning of the most economical way of placing the pattern pieces on the fabric, and the preparation of the required number of layers of fabric to be cut at one time. This will depend on the thickness of material used and, obviously, the size of the order.

For instance, when the particular suit illustrated was made, 40 layers of fabric were cut together, involving 80 complete suits (one up and one down the grain of the fabric—which is usually found to be the most economical lay so long as the fabric does not have a pile or a design that can only be used one way).

The pattern pieces, now marked out on heat-seal paper or stuck on with special spray-adhesive, adhere to the top layer of fabric whilst the lay is cut with an electric cutting machine. The pieces are cut with exact seam and hem allowances, but where necessary such things as dart or pocket positions on the individual pieces are marked, either by marking machine or by hot drill, both of which will mark right through the entire lay. Linings, canvases or inter-linings are cut at the same time. The work is then bundled up and ticketed, ready to be distributed to the various operators.

Small parts such as flaps, welts, patch pockets, collars and sleeves are made first. If any of these are to be trimmed with braid, this is done now, but if collars and revers are braided it will be done at a later stage. Wherever edges are sewn, edge trimmers which sew and trim a uniform edge in one operation are used.

Meanwhile, in other sections, the backs and linings are being sewn up and prepared. The seaming of the backs, and also that of the fronts, will include taping the armholes and any other parts that are liable to stretch or which need to be controlled during the making up. The method used for making the fronts will depend on styling, as well as on the preference of the manufacturer. They can either be canvased by plonker machine or interlined, possibly with fusible interlining. At this stage piped buttonholes are made with a piped buttonhole machine.

As the parts are completed they are pressed, either by hand-operated steam electric irons or by pressing machines, some of which are shaped like the contours of the body. The fronts and collars are inspected and checked, prior to assembly.

All parts are now ready for 'closing'—the sewing up of all the main seams of the jacket and the sewing in of collar and sleeves, after which all these seams are pressed.

The edges are basted by basting machine, and then the tailors take over to do whatever is necessary in the way of finishing off lapels, fastening down collar seams and turning up hems at the bottom of jacket and sleeves. The hems are now fastened by blind stitching machine, after which the whole jacket is machine pressed. If collar and revers, front edges or jacket bottom are to be trimmed with braid it will be done now.

At this stage, the linings which have already been prepared are sewn in. The jacket then goes to the tailors who will put in pads and baste the linings at bottoms and cuffs, and then on to the felling machines and hand workers for felling.

The top pressers give the jacket a final pressing by hand before it goes to the cleaners who remove any cottons that might have been overlooked. The button positions are marked and the jacket goes to the finishers who sew on by hand buttons, labels, and any bows or loops or anything else appertaining to the style. At the final passing, if necessary, the pile is freshened with a steam gun.

The skirts, which were cut at the same time as the jackets, are made up simultaneously, the order of work being as follows:

All seams are overlocked by machine to prevent fraying. At this stage some skirts are lined. The seams and darts are machined and the zips put in, sometimes with a special zip machine. If the lining has not already been put in, that is done now. After the skirt measurements have been checked, petersham to size is machined on, followed by a cloth waistband to cover the petersham. The seams are pressed, the bottom is straightened and overlocked, and the hem is turned up and felled by a blind stitching machine known as a feller. After the skirt has been pressed on a specially shaped skirt machine the waistband is finished by the addition of hooks and bar tacks, button and buttonhole or trouser-type clips.

Then comes the final passing and marrying with jackets by means of control tickets, ready for dispatch.

The procedure of manufacturing coats is identical to that of jackets until after the assembly of all parts. Then the coats are basted by machine where necessary, and the tailors do any appropriate hand work. The bottoms are checked, straightened and overlocked, basted and bluffed, a bluffer being a blind stitching machine which fastens up the hem with a long chain stitch.

The coat is then pressed and the lining put in, just as in the jacket, except that it is machined up at the bottom and left loose, attached only by chain loops to the coat hem in a few places. After going to the top pressers, the cleaners and the finishers, the coat goes to be finally passed.

77 There are fewer steps involved in **the production of an average dress** than in the making of a tailored garment, so production costs are considerably lower. Problems in regard to both fabrics and execution are naturally more varied. The following procedure is typical in a firm producing an enormous number of dresses, quickly:

The design arrives at the factory, having been made up by the designers in their own workroom. It is examined, discussed and adjusted where necessary—fit, mass-production technique, saleability and hanger-appeal all being taken into consideration.

Then the pattern is cut and the production plan worked out. A pattern sample is made up, tried on and altered where necessary. Repeat samples are made for travellers. The patterns are graded for sizes and given out to subsidiary contract factories, who each make up samples to be checked before production can be started.

The lay is prepared; this can consist of anything up to 200 layers of fabric if very fine, but is more usually in the realm of 100 in lightweight summer fabrics, 70 in heavier or winter ones. After cutting, any marking is done. Sometimes fusible interlinings are applied at this stage before the work is bundled, ticketed and sent to the machinists. The bundles usually consist of all the pieces for about six garments, including trimmings, interlinings, linings and any decorative work which has been done outside.

Most firms today favour the make-through principle—that is, each machinist sewing up the entire dress before it is checked and passed on to the overlockers. After overlocking, sleeves and bottoms are turned up and hemmed by feller. At this stage any buttonholes are made (stitched rather than piped, which will eliminate hand finishing) and the buttons are attached, usually by machine.

Any appropriate hand finishing is done next, after which the dress is hand pressed. The cottons are trimmed off, the dress is checked, and swing tickets and coloured size tabs are put on to facilitate allocation.

All dresses, including those from the outside contract factories, are taken to the central warehouse where every garment is finally checked and passed, ready for allocation and dispatch.

78 It seems logical to me that **if a machinist in a factory can make several garments in a day it should not be beyond the capabilities of the individual dressmaker to work through all the various procedures involved in the making of a fairly simple garment, provided that no fitting is required, and produce a thoroughly satisfactory result in a matter of a very few hours**. This is assuming that she knows how to operate her machine fast and efficiently and has had some previous experience of the various techniques involved. In planning the order of work thought must be given to the amount and the type of inside finish required, some methods—pinking, binding and overlocking for example—being done at the cutting out stage, other—french seams, flat felling, top-stitching, over-sewing amongst them—at the appropriate time during the making up. Whilst there is undoubtedly much self satisfaction in finishing a garment beautifully inside, presumably no-one is going to see this apart from maker-up and wearer. My own view is that the finishing should be appropriate to the type of fabric and the expected life of the garment, strengthening seams and preventing them from fraying, ensuring that no loose ends hang down and, in the case of some man-made fibre fabrics that will not press flat, stitching them so as to avoid that otherwise inevitable bulbous appearance. It would appear that pinking is the perfect finish for plastic-coated fabrics whereas thick, rough tweed raw edges would be better bound, for example.

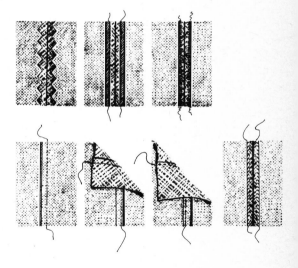

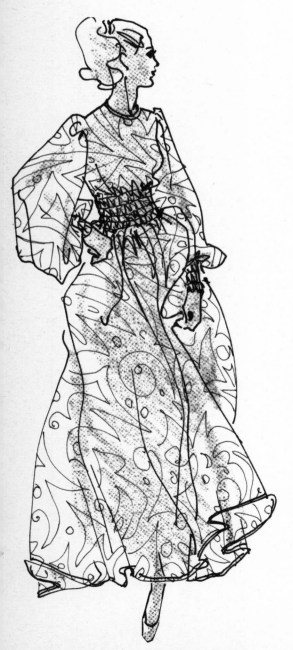

79 In many cases, of course, **lining** would be the most satisfactory method of all to finish the inside of a garment, rendering unnecessary specific seam neatening. But lining can serve many other purposes besides:

*Warmth—of the lining itself and/or by helping to trap a layer of warm air for insulation.
*Comfort, particularly where the garment is made of hard or scratchy or hairy fabric.
*'Slip'; we all know how difficult it is to pull on an unlined garment over another.
*Decency, for those parts of a garment not meant to be see-through.
*Strength; apart from reinforcing delicate fabrics, by providing 'slip' lining considerably reduces the stresses and strains imposed when a garment is being pulled on and off as well as during active wear.
*'Body'; lining automatically makes a flimsy garment more substantial.
*Dimensional stability; even an unbonded lining can do much to support a garment and keep it in good shape where it might otherwise sag.

80 It is important to **choose the appropriate lining**, the right weight and type and colour:

*Too thick a lining will show through the outer fabric, too thin and it will wear out in no time.
*In general, man-made linings are best with man-made fabrics, natural ones with natural fabrics.
*A matching lining will avoid any possibility of the slightest colour change on the outside between single and double layers of the garment—areas such as, for example, facings, pockets, hems and seam turnings. Many quite substantial fabrics are not as opaque as one might expect.
*If an outer garment is to be worn over darker clothing, or garments likely to be soiled during normal wear, a dark-coloured lining is clearly a wiser choice than a pale one; in the case of the lining colour showing through the outer fabric an *interlining* is necessary.
*Garments can be wholly or part-lined. Part-lining is only satisfactory where the main fabric is truly opaque; it can take the place of facings, especially where these would prove bulky—(*facings* can be made from lining fabric)—and helps prevent seating in the back of skirts.

81 For the sake of decency **transparent fabrics must be lined**; the unattractively patchy look of a part-lined dress is avoided if a flesh-coloured lining is used rather than one which matches the main fabric. Then if all seams and hems are as narrow as possible and the dress only worn over flesh-coloured undergarments the effect will be delicately filmy and totally decent—and the essential charcter of the fabric exploited to the full.

70

82 Preserving **the essential character of beautiful fabrics**, using materials with understanding and appreciation, using them excitingly but never unsuitably—these are the hallmarks of a good designer. Some fabrics are works of art in themselves, beautiful prints, complicated weaves or intricate blends of colours and fibres which 'speak' to the designer who knows exactly what to do with them the moment he or she sets eyes on them. Obviously heavily patterned or textured materials are best made up in uncomplicated designs, the over-all effect being achieved by silhouette and fabric rather than by detail or by intricate seaming or darting which, unless they had the virtue of more subtly shaping the garment, would be completely wasted. A good basic rule is: elaborate fabric—simple garment design. (The corollary, however, rarely applies; whilst simplicity in design is nearly always considered a virtue, elaboration generally is not.)

New fashions are often inspired by fabrics. One year these may be bulky, another smooth and flat; one season they might drape and cling, the next stand crisply away from the figure or float softly about it. Sometimes the feeling is for floral or abstract prints, plaids, checks, herringbones, stripes or spots; sometimes the interest is all in the surface texture—nubbly flecks, bouclés, crepes or ribbed, hairy or fluffy fabrics. There are times when a particular fabric will disappear completely from the fashion scene to reappear several years later, possibly improved, to provide fresh stimulation and inspiration for the designer.

Faced with the enormous range of fabrics made from all the natural and man-made fibres available today, many factors must be taken into account by the designer, amongst them weight, handle, price, performance in wear, behaviour during manufacturing processes or making up, suitability for designs, suitability for prospective clients, suitability for climate and season as well as the most obvious factor of all—appearance—which includes colour, pattern, weave and texture.

About most fabrics made from natural fibres one could say that that they have an excellent 'handle' and 'feel'. They absorb and dispel moisture easily, which makes them comfortable to wear in extreme or changeable climates, and they age gracefully, still looking good when no longer brand new. In use, almost all textile fibres are subject to friction, acquiring small charges of static electricity which attract dust particles from the atmosphere— one of the ways in which garments become soiled. This static electricity accumulates much less readily on natural fibres, so yet another advantage is that they tend to stay clean longer.

Wool is probably the most versatile of all textile fibres used in the clothing industry. It can be spun and woven into cloths which weigh anything from 105 to 1350 grammes per metre, and can be manufactured and finished in the widest possible variety of ways

71

such as worsted, facecloth, velour, boucle, fur fabric, chiffon, jersey, felt and lace. It is therefore suitable for all seasons and climates and for any occasion. It can also be printed or jacquard-woven into patterns or into a variety of checks, plaids, stripes and fancy weaves. The finished cloth can be smooth and glossy, soft and fluffy, coarse and shaggy, light and lacy, firm and nubbly. Wool is probably the favourite fabric of all tailors and dressmakers who make garments by hand, being easy and pleasant to work and, like no other fabric, it can be moulded and shrunk by steam pressing to a required shape—for instance, round the head of a sleeve in a tailored garment—to give a smooth finish without puckering. This quality also makes an absolutely perfect finish inside a garment, any unwanted fullness at seams or hems being pressed away. And it is mainly the reason why, together with its natural warmth and sympathetic handle, wool is especially suited to blending with other fibres, both natural and man made.

The natural elasticity of wool enables clothes to recover their shape after wearing (should they have lost it in the first place). Whilst absorbing and dispelling moisture given off by the body in the form of perspiration, wool fabrics are at the same time naturally water-repellent—as is the sheep, after all—so if the wearer of woollen outer garments is caught in a light shower the chances are that she will be able to shake off any spots of rain.

Woollen fabrics can now be treated so as to be permanently moth-proof, showerproof and/or stainproof. They can also be permanently pleated, 'set' so that they shed accidently gained creases even faster than normally, and given hand or machine-washable shrink resistant finishes. Because wool carries no static electricity it is free from 'sparkling' and does not attract dust and dirt from the atmosphere.

Cotton fabrics for clothes are usually particularly fresh and attractive in appearance as well as comfortable in wear, especially in hot weather. They are simple and rewarding to launder—can be boiled if necessary, so long as the dyes are fast. Cotton materials are extremely easy to sew and pleasant to handle when making up, being unlikely to slip or fray. They can be treated to repel water and to resist shrinking and staining. They can also be made flame-resistant.

Cotton fibres can be bleached, mercerised (a process which strengthens them and imparts a fine lustrous sheen), made into fabrics with plain or fancy weaves, knitted, printed, embossed, brushed to raise a nap, made into pile fabrics, into stretch fabrics, backed with foam or treated with crease-resisting easy-care finishes.

Some of the many cotton fabrics available are: lawn, voile, polished cotton, satin, gingham, pique, sailcloth, denim, poplin, seersucker, terry towelling, velvet, gabardine, doeskin, Bedford cord, fancy-woven suiting, corduroy and lace; even from this short list one realizes how versatile a fibre cotton is and how wide is the range of garments for which cotton fabrics can be used.

Linen fabrics have a beautiful sheen and air of quality. They are the coolest of all—even cooler than cottons—for wear in hot climates. They have a long life and stand up well to repeated laundering, due to their high tensile strength when wet. The one great disadvantage, creasing, has been largely overcome by subjecting the cloth to a crease-resisting process and also, in many cases, by blending with a proportion of man-made fibres. Crease recovery is much improved by blending with 25% Polyester fibre; when combined with $66\frac{2}{3}\%$ linen will take permanent pleating whilst still retaining in many cases its appearance, feel and other advantages.

Linen and linen blends are obtainable as stretch fabrics, printed, machine embroidered, in a variety of novelty weaves or plain (its texture being one of the features of linen). Couturiers have used also finely pleated handkerchief linen to make beautiful evening separates.

Most people would agree that, with the possible exception of vicuna, there is no more luxurious fibre in the world than **silk**. It is cool in summer, warm in winter, lightweight, finely textured and, properly cared for, long-lasting too. Silk fabrics are often naturally crease-resisting and always wonderfully comfortable to wear, there being nothing to equal the feel of them next to the skin.

Silk is available in the form of many different fabrics suitable for all occasions; there are washing silks for everyday wear—plain or printed shantung, tussor, spun silk and colour woven fabrics. Jap silk makes a perfect lining for most garments made from natural fabrics. For more formal afternoon or evening wear, depending on what sort of effect is required—stiff and bouffant or clinging and draped—there are masses of beautiful silk fabrics from which to choose, amongst them crêpe-de-Chine, printed surah, silk tweed, papillon, tulle, taffeta, velvet, faille, wild silk, organza, grosgrain, Thai silk, duchess satin, brocade . . . As well as all these, blends such as silk and wool, silk and Acrilan, silk and Terylene, silk and rayon, and silk and nylon exist, which combine all the qualities of the two fibres and consequently widen still further the scope for the designer.

83 **Designs using luxurious fabrics or substances need not work out prohibitively expensive**. Clever use of the chosen material *combined with other, cheaper fabrics* can put exotic-looking clothing withing the reach of the majority of women. Basically the idea is to get maximum capital from the material to be featured by situating it where it will show most, wear least and not be cut about wastefully. (The cleaning and maintenance of the two fabrics will have to be compatible if this is not to cause complications at a later date.) Consider designs that have an unbroken area down the centre front and/or across the top of the bodice, or around the neckline, along the shoulders . . . Any separately made details or the 'small parts' referred to in the section on mass-production might be made in the luxury material—or small sections, cleverly designed as part of the construction to be incorporated during the making up. Whilst making the best and most economical use of expensive materials the designs can, when dealing with difficult-to-handle fabrics, be devised for ease of manufacture; for instance, edges in fluffy or pile fabrics can be sandwiched between two layers of some smooth-surfaced fabric or substance, or encased in ready-folded braid, inserting a centre front zip being a simple procedure with easy-to-handle flat fabrics—but not so with rough, flimsy, uneven or pile fabrics.

84 Although not strictly 'cloth' here seems the appropriate place to include two other natural fibres used in the fashion industry, **leather** and fur—certainly they come into the luxury class whilst also being, in the majority of cases, highly functional and practical. The words 'leather', 'suede' and 'sheepskin' convey to the general public a clear picture of three separate entities, but since they all have a common origin the use of these terms is not strictly correct. Few people outside the trade realize that practically all skins used for clothing come from the sheep. After careful preliminary selection as to suitability the final surface effect is achieved (after tanning) by the finishing of one side or the other of the skin. **Grain leather** is the skin or outer surface from which all wool or hair has been removed whereas **suede leather** is usually the flesh or inner surface, finished with a velvet-like nap. **Woolled sheepskin** is the whole skin which has been tanned and dressed with the wool on.

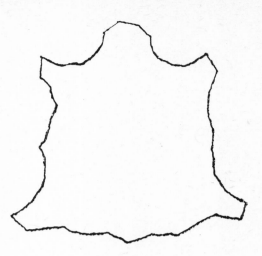

The designer of any garment in leather has always to keep in mind one fundamental limitation—the size of the usable parts of the skin. Some skins *are* bigger than others, but the body of any garment larger than the average jacket will inevitably have a join across it somewhere and it is the job of the designer to see that these joins enhance rather than detract from the appearance—to make it seem that they are there by choice. Because leather cannot be shrunk, stretched or otherwise moulded by the maker-up all shaping must be in the cut. And, as cleaning is expensive and not always satisfactory designs should be smooth, without any bumpy gathers or pleats which would quickly catch the dirt and show signs of wear long before the rest of the garment.

Leather is not cheap but it has many qualities to recommend it, not least a marvellous 'feel' and natural beauty. Long-lasting, lightweight and weather-proof it can, unlike fur, be worn the year round. If classically styled and not too closely-fitted it will not date, and, something that cannot be said for most synthetic substances, properly cared for it will still retain its good looks when very obviously no longer new.

As it can be dyed any conceivable colour, and with few limitations be stitched and worked like cloth, it is perfectly feasible to manufacture garments in leather for every conceivable occasion; but since it is after all a protective substance leather is always at its practical, beautiful best made up as classic coats and jackets and garments for casual and sportswear, preferably when in the more natural-seeming colours from black, through all shades of brown, to beige (natural-seeming' because *all* skins for clothing are dyed). There seems little point in trying to compete with fabrics in fields where by their very nature fabrics are more suitable, for instance as dresses for evening or party wear or as gimmick clothes intended for one short season only.

78

Leather deserves styling that takes into account its unique qualities and uses them to advantage, at its best trimmed or teamed with other animal derivatives such as wool, silk or fur—or other types or colours of leather. It combines attractively with, for example, jerseys and suitings but designers of garments for mass-production can rarely allow themselves the pleasure of creating ensembles such as, for instance, a grain leather trimmed tweed suit with matching fabric-lined leather jacket, or perhaps a suede leather and jersey jerkin over jersey dress teamed with suede three-quarter coat since few manufacturers have the facilities and the skilled workers to produce both leather *and* fabric clothes; also each leather garment is necessarily 'bundled' right from the start, meaning that it has been individually cut from carefully matched skins—matched according to colour, weight and texture—and these pieces stay together as they go through the various processes of manufacture until they emerge as a finished garment. The manufacture of fabric garments being a far speedier and less individual process altogether, it would obviously be uneconomic to try to combine the two types of production unless there were a worthwhile market. (Cleaning may cause problems too, a point to watch out for.) Unfortunately ensembles of any sort are rarely to be found in stores because of the sharp divisions into which buying for the various departments falls—suits, dresses, coats, blouses . . . But there is great scope for the individual designer and maker-up—as well as for the home dressmaker—the techniques for making clothes in leather are easily learnt; plenty of books are available on the subject. The processes certainly take longer, entailing much pounding and sticking, but the resulting garments do last a long time.

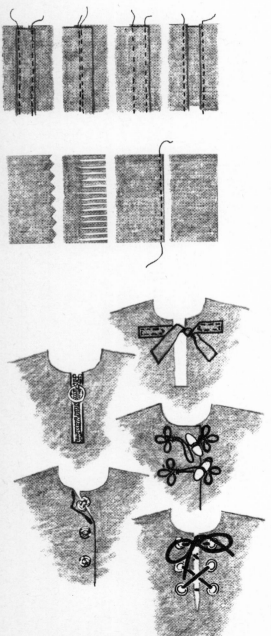

A few general points to remember when designing leather garments:

*Avoid buttonholes in seams where possible as they tend to weaken the structure of the seams.

*Straight skirts inevitably 'seat' a little in wear and cannot be pressed and shrunk back into shape as can most fabrics; gently flared skirts are altogether more satisfactory, both from the point of view of wearer and of the manufacturer for the mass market, who can achieve a better fit that way for a wider variety of fittings.

*Leather garments for children, although charming, and practical too, in the form of coats, jackets, pinafore dresses, skirts and trousers, tend to be almost as expensive to produce as full-size garments as they have to go through all the same processes. Because it keeps clean longer, grain rather than suede leather seems the obvious choice but the amount of wear a fast-growing child will get out of any expensive item of clothing is a relevant factor.

*In the making of woolled sheepskin coats and jackets seams are preferable to darts for shaping as darts spoil the look of the inside.

*The edges of this type of garment can be turned and top-stitched but the better, though more expensive, way is to bind them with leather.

*If the stitching round the pocket shape is going to show on the outside (and this certainly makes a neater job on the *inside*) make sure that the lines fit harmoniously with other lines of the design.

*Stitching on leather is traditional, and can be an important decorative feature; saddle stitching has to be done by hand and is therefore expensive; so too is the finishing of an edge by means of pressing and sticking—machining is a cheaper alternative.

*Top-stitching seams makes them into an attractive feature and strengthens them at the same time.

Some modern designs, as a rule made from rough-surfaced suede leathers, actually incorporate several economical features whilst looking casually, elegantly expensive. Strap, tuck, flat-felled and channel seams, all with raw edges exposed, are often used. Edges may be pinked, fringed, top-stitched or simply left raw; fastenings are usually exposed zips, ties, frogging, press fasteners, eyelets and lacings; buttonholes need be no more than slits reinforced with stitching and the garments may even be unlined.

Designs can be created to use a number of small sections, resulting in a more economical cut than is otherwise possible with leather clothing. Grain and suede leather combine attractively in the same garment; from the practical point of view in any case, because it keeps clean longer, it is a good idea to use grain leather strategically in the places most likely to soil—around neck, sleeve, pocket and front edges.

As a point of interest and to prove how a good leather design is unlikely to date the garments here are those designed for inclusion in *The Technique of Dress Design*, first published in 1966.

85 With the possible exception of evening wraps, the wearing of **fur** is seasonal, confined to the cooler months of the year. Certainly fur garments are expensive in comparison with their fabric counterparts but they possess wonderful qualities of warmth, great beauty and a superb 'feel' combined with the fact that they can do more to flatter a woman's skin, enhance her looks and impart the pleasurable sensation of pampered luxury than can practically any fabric.

On top of the cost of the skins themselves there is a shortage of skilled workers, increasingly highly paid whilst at the same time more and more difficult to attract into the industry—a familiar story these days.

As with leather clothing, designs for fur must take into account the size and shape of the skins. The furrier can join, stretch, narrow or widen furs such as mink, sable, squirrel, fox and ermine in any manner required by the design, but the very separateness of each skin gives garments in these furs their distinctive character.

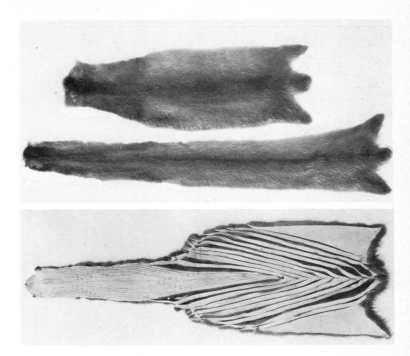

Illustrated here is one of the processes involved in the making of most garments in beaver, mink, musquash and sable—stranding. As well as showing how skins are lengthened it also shows one of the reasons why coats in these furs are so expensive, all this cutting and machining having to be hand-done by highly skilled operators. Below the couture level some stranding machines are used, but they are in any case only suitable for large skins such as beaver. These have a subtle natural shading and are generally stranded to lengthen the skin for making into full-length coats, thereby avoiding having seams across the garment; beaver skins worked otherwise would be too wide and due to their shading, somewhat characterless. Some furs—mink, sable and fox for example—can be worked round instead of down, either stranded (which will work out just as expensive) or not. In the case of non-stranded skins there will probably be joins at the under-arm seam, and certainly down the centre back, the average mink or sable skin being only 48-60 cm long.

Although fusible tapes and interlinings might play some part in the making of fur garments many processes will always have to be done by hand, amongst them cutting, nailing, lining and, particularly in the case of wild animals, any necessary repairing of the pelts; skins, of course, need to be exactly matched as to colour, quality, and, where appropriate, markings.

83

Obviously a woman who can only afford to have one fur garment at a time in her wardrobe is likely to choose a fairly classic design in a hard wearing fur which she will be able to wear on as many occasions as possible. Depending, naturally, on their quality, hard-wearing furs include otter, mink, persian lamb, musquash and beaver lamb. This latter is none other than the versatile sheepskin tanned and processed in yet another guise. Furs not likely to wear so well—although this again depends on their quality—include broadtail, ermine, some types of rabbit (usually referred to as 'coney'), squirrel and nutria.

The individual dressmaker can learn to make up skins into garments, but the process is a lengthy one mainly consisting of joining skins together by means of oversewing on the pelt side, strengthening, padding and interlining. It should not be overlooked that beautiful fur fabrics are made today that are easy to make up and almost indistinguishable from the real thing. For economy, why not a fur fabric coat with a real fur collar and cuffs, for example?

Designs for fur should be both flattering and practical, any garments outside that description being only for women who can afford costly gimmicks. This branch of the fashion industry certainly offers scope for good ideas, the more so as men take to wearing fur coats and as skin merchants look around for more variety in the raw materials. Calfskin and hamster are being used interestingly, mink looks good combined with knitting or leather; patchy, uneven-patterned furs combine well with smoother-surfaced single-coloured furs—or leather. Seal, otter, pony and calfskin go well with fox, badger or mink.

Although many older women are likely to prefer their furs to be face-framing and adaptable, useful for both day and evening, designs these days tend to be more casual—less full and with narrower sleeves and smaller collars. Copies of classic cloth garments in particular are outstandingly chic, flattering to all ages.

Again, with the aim of showing that a good fur design is unlikely to date, readers may recognize that the designs here are the same as those in *The Technique of Dress Design* and were therefore produced sometime before 1966.

86   It is mainly due to the advances made by the **man-made fibres** industries that the sort of clothes which look to all intents and purposes like those formerly worn only by wealthy women with personal maids whose job it was to help maintain their fabulous appearance, are now within the reach of all. Many of these modern, often incredibly reasonably-priced garments can be washed, drip-dried overnight and put on again next day without further attention. The changes that have taken place in the wardrobe of the average woman are well known and need no elaboration here.

All was not quite so marvellous in the early days. **Rayon**, the first man-made fibre—and now in its many forms the most widely used of all (in many other branches of the textile industry as well as fashion)—and **acetate**, the second, became familiar to the general public as 'artificial silk' and although economically a blessing to most, were automatically regarded as somewhat inferior substitutes for the real thing. **Nylon**, the third man-made fibre to come on to the market, was not at first the answer to the fashion industry's prayers either, the earliest fabrics being uncomfortable to wear next to the skin, mainly because the fibre did not absorb moisture.

Since those early days, though, the picture has changed completely. Today all three have an entirely different public image and it would be difficult to imagine life without them. Any former disadvantages have been largely overcome or counteracted by one means or another and most fabrics made from them and other man-made fibres are good enough to stand in their own right, even considered by many an improvement on natural fibre fabrics. Certainly any new fabric put on the market today that is not comfortable to wear and satisfactory in performance stands a poor chance of success.

Most man-made fibres possess at least some of the following qualities:
*easy-care and maintenance, which often includes washability
*resistance to damage by moths
*resistance to unintentional creasing and, once woven or knitted into fabrics,
*dimensional stability—holding their shape without shrinking or stretching. In addition many of these fabrics are
*inexpensive
*light in weight
*need little or no ironing and
*hold permanent pleats.

One disadvantage of some man-made fibres is the tendency, due to the accumulation of static electricity, to attract dust particles more readily than natural fibres, but most consider this is largely offset by their easy-care qualities and can usually be successfully, if temporarily, counteracted by the use of fabric 'softeners'. There is, too, a tendency for some fabrics to cling to the body for the same reason. Another disadvantage is that many man-made fibres are non-absorbent; however, some of them have an irregular structure which enables them to act like a wick, transferring moisture away from the body so that it can evaporate. Others, made into fabrics with a fairly open structure, allow air to circulate and are consequently more comfortable to wear. Yet others are crimped and bulked so that when woven or knitted they will retain little pockets of air and so give insulation without weight in both warm and cool conditions and have a soft handle.

By the time most fibres have been developed and rigorously tested their behaviour is, or should be, predictable under all circumstances; no one man-made fibre has all the advantages, but by combining two or more into one yarn or one fabric, it is possible to utilize the advantages of each whilst counteracting their disadvantages. They are often blended with natural fibres too, as noted earlier, frequently resulting in highly satisfactory, reasonably priced fabrics which give excellent performance both during manufacture and in wear.

There seems no doubt that competition between natural and the man-made fibre industries has resulted in improvements to both and consequently, advantages to the general public; nowadays dimensionally stable, washable and hard-wearing, good-looking cloths are taken for granted.

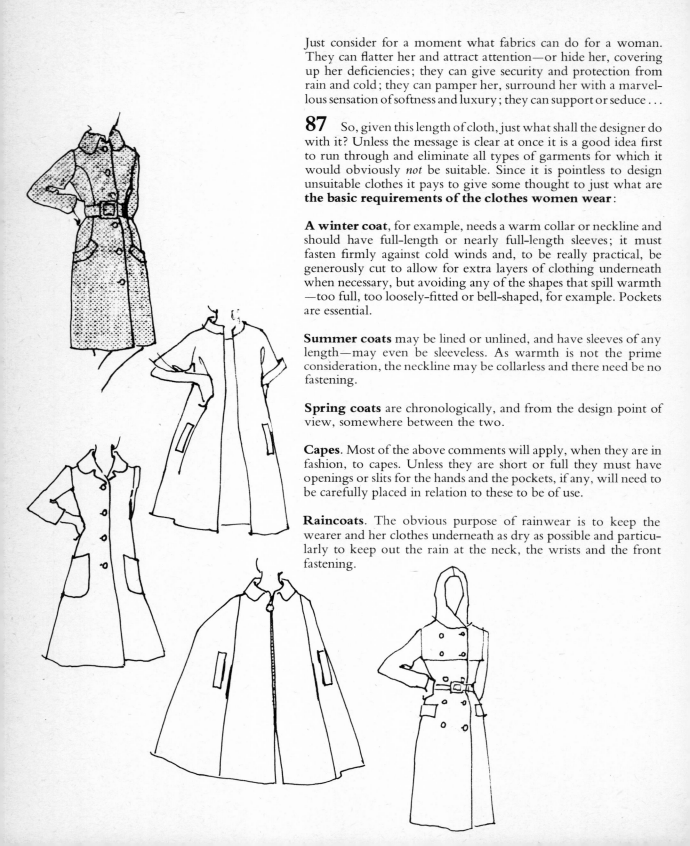

Just consider for a moment what fabrics can do for a woman. They can flatter her and attract attention—or hide her, covering up her deficiencies; they can give security and protection from rain and cold; they can pamper her, surround her with a marvellous sensation of softness and luxury; they can support or seduce . . .

87   So, given this length of cloth, just what shall the designer do with it? Unless the message is clear at once it is a good idea first to run through and eliminate all types of garments for which it would obviously *not* be suitable. Since it is pointless to design unsuitable clothes it pays to give some thought to just what are **the basic requirements of the clothes women wear**:

A winter coat, for example, needs a warm collar or neckline and should have full-length or nearly full-length sleeves; it must fasten firmly against cold winds and, to be really practical, be generously cut to allow for extra layers of clothing underneath when necessary, but avoiding any of the shapes that spill warmth —too full, too loosely-fitted or bell-shaped, for example. Pockets are essential.

Summer coats may be lined or unlined, and have sleeves of any length—may even be sleeveless. As warmth is not the prime consideration, the neckline may be collarless and there need be no fastening.

Spring coats are chronologically, and from the design point of view, somewhere between the two.

Capes. Most of the above comments will apply, when they are in fashion, to capes. Unless they are short or full they must have openings or slits for the hands and the pockets, if any, will need to be carefully placed in relation to these to be of use.

Raincoats. The obvious purpose of rainwear is to keep the wearer and her clothes underneath as dry as possible and particularly to keep out the rain at the neck, the wrists and the front fastening.

Evening coats can be any appropriate length down to the floor. They are usually made in glamorous materials, and can be extravagant or simple in design, with or without fastening, and with sleeves of any length. (There are alternatives to coats for wearing over evening dresses—stoles, capes, jackets, waistcoats . . .)

Suits can be for almost any occasion, season, type or age-group, designed with straight or full skirts, sleeves or no sleeves, can be made to fasten or not, have any type of collar or neckline, be designed to wear with or without a blouse, sweater or waistcoat, and can be made in any fabric; a suit is basically a two-piece—a jacket of any length and a skirt, or trousers.

Dresses too can vary as widely as suits. Generally speaking, for winter they should be made in warm materials with warm sleeves and warm necklines and they should not be enormously full-skirted, mainly because of the bulk and weight of the majority of winter fabrics. However, this kind of dress is not very practical for those who live in centrally heated houses or work in centrally heated offices, so also for winter we have dresses still probably made in wool or bulked man-made fibre fabrics, but with short or no sleeves and with cooler necklines, sometimes teamed with matching jackets, cardigans or over-blouses. Dresses for summer are made in cooler, smoother fabrics, and vary between those suitable for town—straightish, often with sleeves and reasonably high necklines, probably made up in darker materials or prints which do not readily show dirt—and those unsuitable for town (but alas, all too frequently seen there) with huge skirts, no sleeves, low backs, and low fronts made in the palest or in the most startlingly vivid colours possible. In between the extremes of summer and winter come all the obvious variations of design and fabric called for by changeable climates and the differing needs of varied populations.

'Cocktail dresses'. Styles of entertaining being so diverse these days, clothes worn for parties are wonderfully varied. Simply remember that most parties take place in hot, overcrowded rooms and design according to the likely tastes of the wearer. The neckline of a typical cocktail dress is often cut low and/or decorated to flatter. It can be sleeveless—need have no more than shoulder straps, in fact. So long as the shape of the dress is right, fabrics can be pretty well anything. They can cling, shimmer, sparkle, or simply provide a good, plain background for jewellery. A useful alternative to the cocktail dress is the cocktail suit—a party two-piece, but in this case the fabric *must* be exciting, possibly velvet, glittering jersey, brocade or satin.

Evening wear. At one time there was a marked distinction between *evening* dresses—long, off-the-shoulder, strapless or backless—and *dinner* dresses—still long, but with upper arms and shoulders covered so that the wearer showed a fair amount of dress rather than flesh above the dinner table. Eventually short evening dresses became popular for all but the most formal occasions, to be superseded some years later by a return to long dresses; but these have tended to become more and more informal in style—as have, in general, manners and modes of entertaining. Evening dresses, and trousers too, can be made in an enormously wide range of fabrics, but the designer should always bear in mind that the wearer will want to look her best and prettiest, and that she will probably be dancing in a hot and overcrowded room—and sitting down too from time to time.

Dresses for weddings and important occasions should reflect the more extreme changes of fashion less than other garments as they will probably be photographed and looked at again and again over the years; unless they are later to appear a bit of a joke they are best designed on classical, unexaggerated lines, becoming to the figure but at the same time not revealing too much of it.

93

An ensemble is two or more garments specifically designed to be worn together. They are extremely useful, particularly in an uncertain climate, always imparting to the wearer a well-turned-out look. Unfortunately, they are rarely made by the manufacturers who sell to the stores because of the sharp, admittedly logical, divisions into which the buying for the various departments—suits, coats, dresses, blouses, etc—falls. There are exceptions to this however—the outsize department, for one. . . .

Separates—Under this heading come all those clothes which, whilst not often specifically designed to be worn together, do in fact combine usefully in practice and no woman's wardrobe which did not include a selection of at least some of them—jackets, blouses, skirts, sweaters and cardigans, trousers and waistcoats. **Jackets** can be single or double-breasted—be made to fasten or not; they can have sleeves of any length or be sleeveless, have collars or be collarless, but nearly always they have pockets. Straight or boxy ones generally look best with short skirts, fitted ones with long skirts and trousers. **Blouses** can either be pulled over the head or put on like a jacket and fastened—down the front or the back or along the shoulders. They can be designed to be worn tucked in at the waist or as an over-blouse, with sleeves or without. They can vary between the very dressy and frilly and the plain and strictly tailored shirt, depending on the type of occasion and the time of day, as well as the age and type of the intended wearer. **Skirts** too may be worn at any time of day, ranging from divided skirts or culottes intended mainly for sports wear to skirts for formal evening as well as casual day wear. They can be fitted to the waist, rest on the hip bones or hug the midriff, should allow for easy movement and might have a pocket or two somewhere. Depending on current fashions they may be any length

from well above the knee to the floor. **Sweaters** are always pulled on over the head and are usually intended for day wear, either sporty and casual—possibly knitted in thick, rough-textured or hairy yarn—or for slightly more formal wear in smoother, finer textured yarns. Evening sweaters are usually sleeveless, knitted in fine, soft or possibly fluffy or novelty yarns, sometimes crocheted or all-over patterned, maybe decorated with bead, sequin or machine embroidery or other appropriate trimming. **Cardigans** are either teamed with sweaters as twin sets and designed accordingly, or not, in which case most of the comments on sweaters will apply to them too, except that they are always slipped on like a jacket and are usually fastened with buttons, or occasionally with zips. In recent years cardigans have become high fashion garments, looking particularly good with trousers and long skirts. **Trousers** today are accepted casual wear for women of all ages and sizes. For women who already have more than enough bulk around the hips, the most flattering trousers are those which are not too tight around the waist, and which do not fit too closely elsewhere either; best for most female figures are hipsters which stop short an inch or two below the waist. Cut much longer than formerly, and with a certain amount of flare, trousers look marvellous teamed with long jackets, cardigans or waistcoats. Pockets may be included in the design.

Waistcoats are particularly useful garments. Usually made to match specific outfits, or contrast, they can be in a wide variety of materials. Non-fastening, fastened with buttons or zips, high or low necked, always sleeveless and usually collarless, they are fitted or semi-fitted, sometimes have pockets and may be designed to be worn with or without blouses or sweaters underneath. They can be of any length from a little below the waist or to the floor, and are never tucked into the waistband of skirts or trousers. They hide the join between upper and lower garments, creating a harmonious outfit; they are also one of the best ways of disguising disproportionate figures and concealing figure faults.

Beachwear can include anything from one or two-piece bathing costumes to minute bikinis, usually made in quick-drying stretch fabrics; corsetry techniques, and often padding, ensure for problem figures the best possible shape. Two fabrics, combinations of two or more colours, plains, patterns and trimmings are frequently used to good effect. Whilst the classic bathing costume is always with us, variations and gimmicks come and go—low necks, high necks, high backs, no backs, wide straps, narrow straps, no straps, halter necks, shirring, drapery, skirts, legs, sleeves. . . . Under this same heading come after-swim cover-ups such as stoles, coats, jackets, ponchos, tabards or skirts. The need to comply with local custom regarding beach to hotel wear, as well as protection from too much sun or from chilly breezes, are the factors to bear in mind. Then there is a variety of garments intended for wearing

on the beach or sun terrace. **Sun-dresses**, I maintain, should never have shoulder straps that are not detachable; also, the top of a sun-dress should be a little lower than the top of any other dress a woman is likely to wear, as nothing is uglier than a patchwork of brown and white flesh exposed when she later wears evening or party dress. For beachwear the designer can use vivid and exciting colours, the subtler shades tending to look insipid in bright sunshine. A word about fabric: as these garments are likely to get stained with sun tan oils, it is essential that they wash satisfactorily —cottons are especially suitable as well as being comfortable in hot weather; and do avoid metal trimmings, which can get surprisingly hot in the sun.

Sportswear. As a rule, fashions in sportswear—tennis, golf, sailing, horse-riding, swimming, skating, ski-ing—change fairly slowly; in some cases the change over a number of years is hardly discernable, the sports themselves having changed little; the clothes must above all be comfortable, practical, good-looking and entirely appropriate.

97

Lingerie is the collective term for all the articles of clothing not normally seen in wear outside the home, including those worn underneath top clothes, often when a woman is looking far from her best, first thing in the morning and last thing at night. With the ever increasing use of easy-care fabrics, particularly man-made fibre and drip-dry materials, the most exotic-looking creations have now become completely practical from the wearer's point of view—inexpensive to buy, simple to launder, and hard-wearing into the bargain. **Petticoats** or slips can be full-length or just from the waist down, decoratively trimmed or quite plain, and depending on the garments under which they are intended to be worn, flared, stiffened, straight or clinging. Under petticoats go **pants**— sometimes matching, sometimes not, and ranging from the briefest of briefs to directoire knickers, worn for various degrees of decency, hygiene, warmth and comfort. **Nightdresses** and **pyjamas**, worn when a woman is without the support of either make-up or foundation garments, should enhance, flatter, and in some cases camouflage as much as possible. Fashions in nightwear also change slowly, as a rule. Clearly defined bust shaping is unsuitable as the shape of the breast when lying down is totally different from that when standing up. Comfort is essential and it could be safely said that it is only the very young who will go for brevity and/or gimmicks, whilst older women are more likely to want length, prettiness and warmth. **Dressing gowns** vary between collared, practical, warm ones for winters in non-centrally-heated homes and **negligees**—light, flimsy, pretty garments often teamed with matching nightdresses, worn on occasions when an extra layer is needed for decency's sake, but when warmth is not the main consideration. Dressing gowns *must* fasten—with belt, tie, buttons or zip—and may be any length from the knee down but not so long as to trip up a woman wearing flat slippers. Negligees are usually prettily trimmed and fasten at the neck—possibly with a bow or tie. As a rule cut very full owing to the transparency of the fabric, they are sometimes made in two layers to give a subtly shaded look. Also in this section come **housecoats**, breakfast coats, brunch coats—garments in which a woman can look attractive and adequately clad for a meal, for doing a few household chores before dressing properly for the day, and for opening the front door if necessary. Housecoats are often worn around the home in the evening too, most useful made in pretty, non-transparent, easy-care fabrics, with sleeves either tight or else not longer than three-quarter, a pocket for a handkerchief; they should not, of course, be closely fitted as they too will usually be worn without foundation garments. Breakfast and brunch coats should be short; housecoats may be full-length, but all should fasten securely without gaping down the front and have sleeves that will not dangle into the washing-up water.

Leisure clothes. Today's increasingly casual styles of living and entertaining have given rise to the development of a new way of dressing—leisure clothes, also mainly worn without foundation garments and therefore only really practical in non-transparent fabrics, without precise bust fitting. Sometimes these clothes take the form of truly dual-purpose garments—nightdresses that can just as well be worn to a party, pyjamas that are also perfect for garden or terrace, kaftans to wear to the theatre or as a housecoat. Always they are quick to slip on, comfortable, decent, usually voluminous and long—and always vastly becoming.

Classic clothes cannot be excluded from a list of garment definitions. Made for whatever purpose, they are usually unspectacular in appearance, with no memorable detail or trimming which would detract from their usefulness. The emphasis is always on perfect, unexaggerated cut, usually in the better materials because, after all, their usefulness lies in the fact that they will remain wearable and still look right through many seasons—the reason why classics form the basis of many an elegant woman's wardrobe. They would comply with anybody's definition of safe good taste, being neither fitted nor extreme in any way and even some made many years ago might still, differently accessorized and with the necessary adjustments to length and proportions, look perfectly right today.

A word about gimmick clothes—much beloved by some sections of the media because of their news value; designers or buyers of gimmicks should never forget that a great deal of money can be lost on fleeting crazes, particularly when ill-timed or vulgar; there is, after all, a distinction between 'fun' clothes and funny clothes. This is not to say, though, that there is no place for gimmicks and crazy ideas in the world of fashion today—things which often provide the stimulation without which the garment industry might become awfully dull.

88 But even within these definitions of clothing types a vast range of styles is possible—necessary—for an enormous range of people and circumstances. We all need clothes in order to live our daily lives; well chosen, well designed, they can be a source of pleasure and comfort and support. Now, as never before in history, we are all free to dress as we please. The personal choice of each individual would make a fascinating study that has no place here; however, **analysis will show that every garment consists of at least some of the following elements**:

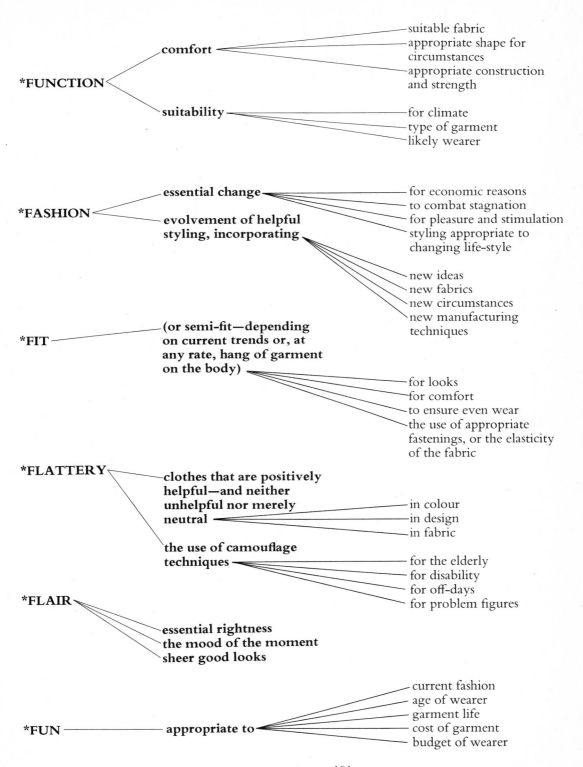

*FUNCTION
- **comfort**
  - suitable fabric
  - appropriate shape for circumstances
  - appropriate construction and strength
- **suitability**
  - for climate
  - type of garment
  - likely wearer

*FASHION
- **essential change**
  - for economic reasons
  - to combat stagnation
  - for pleasure and stimulation
  - styling appropriate to changing life-style
- **evolvement of helpful styling, incorporating**
  - new ideas
  - new fabrics
  - new circumstances
  - new manufacturing techniques

*FIT
- **(or semi-fit—depending on current trends or, at any rate, hang of garment on the body)**
  - for looks
  - for comfort
  - to ensure even wear
  - the use of appropriate fastenings, or the elasticity of the fabric

*FLATTERY
- **clothes that are positively helpful—and neither unhelpful nor merely neutral**
  - in colour
  - in design
  - in fabric
- **the use of camouflage techniques**
  - for the elderly
  - for disability
  - for off-days
  - for problem figures

*FLAIR
- **essential rightness**
- **the mood of the moment**
- **sheer good looks**

*FUN — **appropriate to**
- current fashion
- age of wearer
- garment life
- cost of garment
- budget of wearer

89 **Anyone can design clothes—up to a point—by the simple process of permutation.** Using nothing more than, say, ten necklines, ten basic silhouettes, ten sleeves and ten trimmings it is astounding to realize that without a spark of originality or imagination 10 000 dresses of a sort could be created. Convert those dresses into suits or coats and you have the incredible total of 20 000 garments. Then consider how much the overall appearance of most of them could be altered simply by making them up in different fabrics from the enormous and expanding range available . . .

Clearly, anyone *can* design clothes, but not everyone can automatically be a good designer. This needs flair and experience and the ability to tell good design from bad in one's own work and to sort out the practical from the impractical, together with that instinctive sense of what is right and appropriate for the times and what is not. A good designer has the flair for combining fabrics, textures and colours, for combining fashion with function— fashion without regard for function being ridiculous, function without fashion a wasted opportunity; few women today would consider wearing functional garments that had no relation to current trends.

Fashions stagnate—deteriorate into becoming little more than vehicles for clutter and gimmickry when a particular line stays around for too long, when no good new basic line has evolved. Forced by simple economics couturiers and mass-manufacturers alike have to keep producing a steady flow of garments, at times reduced to shuffling ideas around on the current basic shape. But the vast range of general and specific circumstances remains more or less constant and is always in the mind of the designer. General circumstances will include:
*The likely climate of the country and/or season of the year for which the garment is intended.
*The time of day or the type of occasion when it is most likely to be worn.
*The probable price at which it will sell.
*Any limitations in the method of manufacture to be used.
*The type and age-group of the likely client.

90 **When the design is for an individual client,** as well as her exact type and age-group, her shape and colouring are known, her tastes in clothes and the sort of impression she likes to create, and also whether the outfit is for one special occasion or whether she expects to get a lot of wear out of it. To take some specific examples, such as might come the way of any designer:

Miss A, a young bride-to-be wants a wedding dress and a going-away outfit. Because she has a rather slight, immature figure all designs will need to be worked out over straighter, rather more immature basic figures than usual. Fabrics with a certain amount of body and stiffness which will give a delicate, fresh, youthful impression will probably suit her better than those which cling to the body. Sensibly, she does not wish to spend a great deal of money on a dress that is only going to be worn for a few hours, so a design which could successfully be converted into an evening dress would be a good idea, maybe using fabric that will later dye well. Unlike those elegant pictures in fashion magazines, the photographer will almost certainly pose and photograph the bride from the front, planted squarely on her two feet; an ungimmicky dress, full length and cut on classic lines unlikely to date quickly would seem to be the answer. Modest necklines and covered arms are usually expected at religious ceremonies so if Miss A's dress itself does not meet these requirements as an alternative it could be either low-necked and sleeveless, strapless or with shoulder straps, according to current fashion for evening wear—but worn under matching, back-fastening bolero, or alternatively with some sort of over-blouse also designed to have a useful life after the ceremony; this might be made of lace or chiffon. Backs of wedding dresses being every bit as important as fronts, those with trains look by far the most graceful. Later the dress hem will be taken up appropriately. As for the head-dress, remembering those photographs which will be looked at for years to come, steer clear of anything that looks remotely like fancy dress; if bought separately the client will need to bring it to all fittings. It is important to know too, if they are not being made by the same designer, exactly what the bridesmaids' dresses and head-dresses will be like.

For her going-away outfit, as no-one can predict the weather with certainty, the bride would be best advised to wear an ensemble of some sort—a matching dress and coat or jacket, or trouser outfit made in a colour in which she looks her absolute best, relying mainly on a becoming hat to give her all the appearance of a bride on the day.

Thin and elderly Mrs B just wants some nice clothes for everyday wear. There are several points to remember when designing clothes for the elderly: apart from the more obvious signs such as grey hair and lines and wrinkles on the face, age also shows very much at the neck, shoulders and upper arms. There may be a tendency to stoop and often an increasing lack of mobility, and sometimes actual disablement. Mrs B, being thin, is very sensitive to the cold and always insists on dresses with sleeves at least to the elbow—apart, that is, from one or two of her summer dresses—but even with those she has matching jackets. She lives alone so her clothes must be particularly easy to put on and take off—never back-fastening. Button-through dresses are excellent, as are any clothes she can step into rather than having to pull them over her head. Elderly people usually sit about a good deal, so fabrics must be selected with this in mind. Skirts should not be too tight; pleated, slightly gathered, gored or bias-cut ones would be both suitable and graceful. Two-piece jersey dresses are good; so are dresses with matching cardigan-style jackets and suits with pretty soft blouses. Suits and coats with collars are usually more becoming than those without, owing to that tendency to stoop and appear a little round-shouldered. Mrs B, like most elderly women, likes the feel as well as the look of something soft at the neck—a floppy shiffon bow, a little fur collar, a printed silk tie or an edge of wool ruching. Incidentally, for evening wear, a single layer of lace, net or chiffon covering the arms and shoulders is wonderfully flattering to the skin as well as providing some protection from draughts.

Mrs C is going to take the chair at an important meeting. She is a splendid, large, impressive woman who almost certainly will be wearing a splendid, large, impressive hat on this special occasion. A lot of the effect will—in fact, must—depend on this hat so the rest of the outfit will have to be designed to complement it. As she will almost certainly have some favourite pieces of jewellery she will want to wear—pearls and a brooch at least—this point should be checked and the neckline designed accordingly. A two-piece of some sort in a really stunning colour—dress or jacket or better still, dress and three-quarter or seven-eighths coat, or dress and full-length straight loose coat would be perfect. The fabric must not show any sign of seating or creasing when Mrs C stands up to speak and, most important, the skirt of her dress must be designed so that she can sit easily and unselfconsciously up on the platform.

Mr D is the managing director of an airline and his stewardesses need new uniforms. Before tackling the problem of designing uniforms it is worth while considering why people wear them. Here are some of the reasons: they create a feeling of involvement with organizations engaged in giving service to the public. They instil a sense of pride in appearance without constant concern about it throughout working hours. Those who wear uniforms are immediately recognizable to members of the public who may need their attention. A well-designed uniform, then, should inspire confidence in the ability of the wearer and at the same time be completely suitable for the job being done. The designer needs to know the exact nature and conditions of work of those who will wear them or, if they are for a completely new service, the image or impression to be created. If the uniforms are being changed—why? Are the present ones uncomfortable, old-fashioned, ugly or too like those worn by others? As to the choice of fabrics—a trim, smart appearance with the minimum of maintenance and the maximum of comfort throughout the hours of duty is essential, so the properties of all fabrics should be assessed before the final choice is made, every possible angle being taken into consideration. A further point to remember is that uniforms often have to be worn with comfortable shoes that are not always an asset as regards looks.

Mr D's stewardesses will have been chosen partly for their good appearance so it can be assumed that the designers will not have to worry about disguising problem figures; a versatile ensemble suited to an air stewardess's working conditions is what is needed, bearing in mind the varied climates she will encounter during her hours of duty. A suit seems the obvious choice, teamed with a matching weatherproof coat. Under the jacket there could be an overblouse made in a similar style but with short sleeves; to be worn instead of the jacket in hot climates, made in a washable crease-resisting fabric (and not necessarily in a light or plain colour). A matching apron in that same fabric would complete the outfit, all five garments being trimmed to match—with braid or top-stitching maybe.

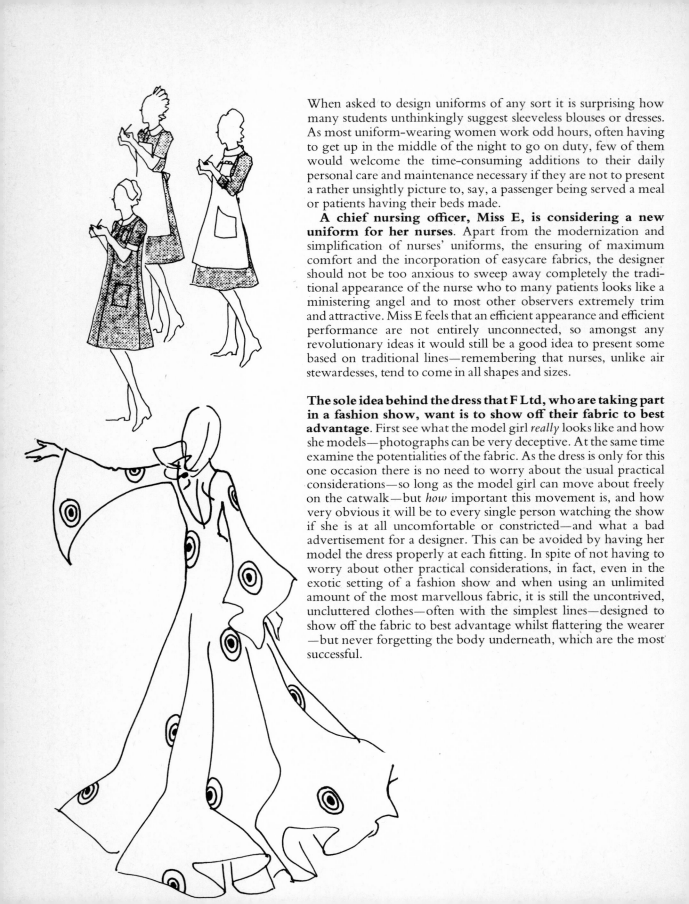

When asked to design uniforms of any sort it is surprising how many students unthinkingly suggest sleeveless blouses or dresses. As most uniform-wearing women work odd hours, often having to get up in the middle of the night to go on duty, few of them would welcome the time-consuming additions to their daily personal care and maintenance necessary if they are not to present a rather unsightly picture to, say, a passenger being served a meal or patients having their beds made.

A chief nursing officer, Miss E, is considering a new uniform for her nurses. Apart from the modernization and simplification of nurses' uniforms, the ensuring of maximum comfort and the incorporation of easycare fabrics, the designer should not be too anxious to sweep away completely the traditional appearance of the nurse who to many patients looks like a ministering angel and to most other observers extremely trim and attractive. Miss E feels that an efficient appearance and efficient performance are not entirely unconnected, so amongst any revolutionary ideas it would still be a good idea to present some based on traditional lines—remembering that nurses, unlike air stewardesses, tend to come in all shapes and sizes.

The sole idea behind the dress that F Ltd, who are taking part in a fashion show, want is to show off their fabric to best advantage. First see what the model girl *really* looks like and how she models—photographs can be very deceptive. At the same time examine the potentialities of the fabric. As the dress is only for this one occasion there is no need to worry about the usual practical considerations—so long as the model girl can move about freely on the catwalk—but *how* important this movement is, and how very obvious it will be to every single person watching the show if she is at all uncomfortable or constricted—and what a bad advertisement for a designer. This can be avoided by having her model the dress properly at each fitting. In spite of not having to worry about other practical considerations, in fact, even in the exotic setting of a fashion show and when using an unlimited amount of the most marvellous fabric, it is still the uncontrived, uncluttered clothes—often with the simplest lines—designed to show off the fabric to best advantage whilst flattering the wearer—but never forgetting the body underneath, which are the most successful.

91 Mrs B's problems were predictable, common to the majority of elderly women; so too are the problems occasioned by overweight and maternity. **The problem of the woman who is big** but well proportioned and possesses good looks and plenty of personality is simply finding clothes that *fit*. With few limitations she should be able to wear any colour and, so long as they are made in her size, most quite normally designed garments. As most large women would agree though, once having found clothes which both fit well and flatter, she would be unlikely to discard them in a hurry, so even this type of woman will choose her wardrobe with care. Garments in the larger size ranges always cost a little more than average ones; for one thing they need more material and for another there are not many manufacturers producing them in the same vast numbers as the average sizes. Distribution is more costly, usually covering a very wide area but at the same time selling fewer garments of a particular style to each shop or store than is possible with the very up-to-the-minute fashion-conscious young styles which have a much quicker turnover.

Outsize garments are made to fit hip measurements of 110 cm (44 inches) and over. As well as being large, the figure may also be unattractive and badly proportioned. The legs and arms—particularly the thighs and upper arms—are usually substantial to say the least and the neck thick and often short (although neck and shoulders *can* be a big woman's best feature, particularly when in evening dress).

At one time it was believed that a vee-neck and a cross-over bodice were the only ways of disguising a large shape. Those days are over, thank goodness. But the solution is not necessarily to clothe that shape in the simplest, plainest possible garments either, however perfectly fitted. The overall shape needs to be broken up a little, the eye drawn inwards away from the silhouette. Designs should be fashionable in trend—after all, many large women are young—but they should not be too showy or gimmicky.

Tight dresses that restrict movement, or those that reveal a bulging or too rigidly corseted figure are bad. In general, avoid closely-fitted tight-waisted skirts, very large prints, horizontal stripes, low waistlines, long jackets and too full sleeves. Lines across the bust are bad, but lines just under the bust are good, particularly if they are slightly shaped, giving a little movement to the design which is flattering to the large figure. (A line under the bust would naturally dispense with the waist seam, any shaping at the waist being given by darts or seams which can be easily altered if necessary to achieve a perfect fit.) Asymmetric lines, diagonal lines and stripes, and bias printed or woven checks are excellent.

The casual look of a dress worn with a straight cardigan-style jacket, or under a tuxedo-fronted seven-eighths coat is excellent because the movement of jacket or coat over the dress will conceal the exact silhouette. Ensembles of any kind are just the thing for the large woman, and the OS department of any store is one place where they will always be found, as well as in most of the 'madam shops'.

A bodice that is draped, or one that is very slightly bloused over a fitted lining is good; so is embroidery, detail or trimming above the bustline or down one side of the bodice.

A straight-fronted skirt with a gored back is liked by some. Some pleated skirts are becoming but should not be too full. A *low* flare provides movement and an illusion of height. Clearly to give an illusion of height in a design by any method means that one automatically takes away from the width.

Face-framing collars, draped or stand-away necklines are flattering to most large women. To break up the figure mass, two tones or colours of the same fabric (in an ensemble perhaps) or two differently textured fabrics in the same colour, such as co-related tweeds, marocain with guipure lace, or a plain linen with a patterned linen which has the same colour background, or velvet with wool crepe could be successful . . .

Strategically placed trimming or detail will always attract the eye from the silhouette, but it must never look as though it has been added as an afterthought (which goes for *any* design, anyway). Most of the work done by outside process specialists can be successfully incorporated.

Fabrics must not add bulk to an already bulky figure *or* reveal it by shining or clinging too closely. Never add to, or reveal the exact outlines of a large mass. Draped printed fine jersey is particularly good for evening and cocktail dresses.

The cut and design of trousers having improved so much in recent years, the majority of big women can look marvellous in modern trouser outfits—and even better in apparently casual trouser ensembles; but the fattest areas *must* be covered by an over-garment—waistcoat or jacket, overblouse or loose shirt—so that eyes are not constantly drawn there; employ camouflage tricks to divert attention elsewhere.

It is on the beach that the OS woman usually finds herself at the greatest disadvantage; generally speaking she looks best when not too much flesh is exposed. Again the casual ensemble is probably most suitable so that even if her sundress is rather too revealing at least she can cover up with a matching jacket or overblouse when she wants to.

It is not possible to make generalization about sleeves because individual preferences vary. Some OS women will happily wear sleeveless dresses, whilst others will only wear garments with sleeves which cover the elbow, or those with three-quarter, bracelet-length or long sleeves. Really full, important sleeves can look marvellous, giving movement and breaking up the bulk. Garments where the length of sleeve is in line with the jacket hem or some other line which goes right across the figure might be unwise and have too widening an effect altogether. But on this point one cannot be dogmatic because with a badly proportioned figure—such as one that is too wide at the hips or too wide at the bust—this very trick might be just what is needed to restore the balance.

OS designs should be drawn over large basic diagrammatic figures to make sure that they really *do* achieve the necessary slimming, flattering effect.

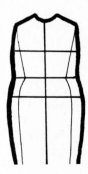

92   Surprisingly to some designers, a pregnant woman is liable to put on weight anywhere, not only around the waistline. Because of endocrine and circulatory changes she is liable to feel the heat more than usual; also, carrying around extra bulk and weight, she may well feel tired and lethargic at times. **Maternity clothes** for her should be as comfortable, morale-building, undemanding and easily maintainable as possible. Whereas formerly their purpose was solely to expand with the wearer whilst attempting to conceal the fact that she was pregnant the advent of the 'trapeze' line and later, 'sack' dresses altered all that; it was realized that these, in addition to being the fashion of the moment, were just about the finest maternity garments ever invented. Since that time the whole attitude of mothers-to-be towards their clothes has changed. The attitude of dress designers towards maternity clothes changed too, and now, instead of being the ugly ducklings of the fashion world, some of the prettiest ready-to-wear clothes available are to be found in the maternity departments of stores and in the many specialist shops that have mushroomed over the last few years—so pretty and flattering in fact that they are frequently bought and worn by women who are not expecting babies.

In the early months of pregnancy though, and possibly, so far as most older women and many career-girl mothers-to-be are concerned, throughout their pregnancies, concealment and camouflage still play an important part. Many of the points relating to designing outsize clothes apply here too.

Not many women will want to buy a large number of special outfits to wear for a comparatively short time, so designs intended for everyday wear need to be both versatile and fairly classical—clothes a woman can dress up or down to suit different occasions and her own personality. Dresses worn under loose, straight coats or jackets, are good—as is anything which helps to break up or obscure the exact outline of the figure. Waistlines, if any, must always be high and gathers or pleats must never splay out over the stomach, drawing attention to it. Pinafore-style dresses that can be worn with or without blouses or sweaters are extremely useful; when designing for a limited wardrobe they are best made in fabrics that will not show every mark, as they are likely to be subjected to almost continuous wear for several months.

Apart from special occasion clothes all fabrics for maternity wear should be easy to maintain, carefully chosen to stand up to hard wear without seating at the back or creasing—particularly across the front under the stomach. Crisp, firm fabrics are better than those which cling closely to the figure; maternity clothes should *never* go in under the bulge.

Well-placed detail or trimming can divert the eye—at least temporarily. Women who are beautiful and confident enough may

111

look their best in completely plain uncluttered dresses, quite regardless of their shape. The majority who are not so fortunate find that such things as flattering necklines, pretty collars, good detail or trimming—placed high up, well away from the stomach—and interesting combinations of two fabrics, two textures and/or two colours can do much for them. Clothes for special occasions and holidays can incorporate some of the ideas and gimmicks of the current season where suitable. Designs for maternity need to be sketched over expectant-looking basic figures.

93 Not so predictable and infinitely more varied are **the problems of the handicapped**, due to the reason for, and degree of, disablement in each individual. The aim of the designer should be towards easy dressing and undressing, comfort as well as a pleasing appearance and the cutting down of need for adjustment and manipulation of the clothing during the day where this is likely to be difficult, painful or impossible without help from others. It may sometimes be that only a partial solution is possible to a clothing problem but since the contemplation of, say, taking two hours to dress oneself *every day* is more than most of us could bear any constructive help is worthwhile. Specially designed or individually made clothing is not necessarily the answer; interest in current fashion and flexibility of outlook can do much to help find solutions, particularly in these days of unprecedented freedom of choice.

Fashion has never before presented us with so many ways to look. Suitably selected off-the-peg garments can provide variety as well as fun and stimulation. Sometimes it will be necessary to adapt and alter them, most often to replace existing fastenings with those which are easier to reach and/or easier to manipulate. To feel that one is dressed in the same mood and manner as everybody else goes a long way towards helping an individual to feel part of the community and many recent fashion trends are particularly suitable for disabled people so long as their attitudes of mind are flexible enough to allow them to experiment. Gone are the days of closely fitted dresses over rigid foundation garments. Casual loose or semi-fitted clothing—often separates—can conceal the silhouette, as well as any lack of support garments.

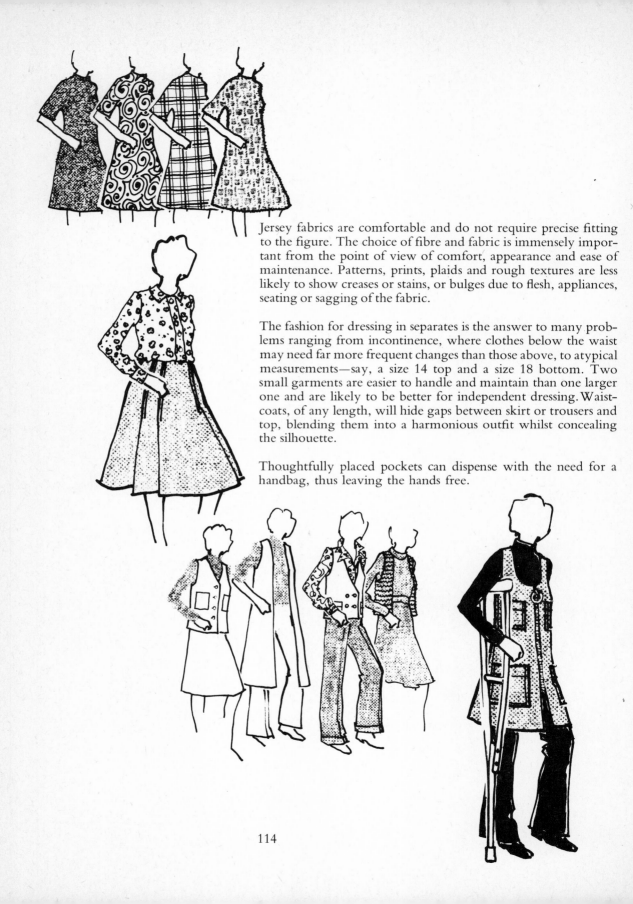

Jersey fabrics are comfortable and do not require precise fitting to the figure. The choice of fibre and fabric is immensely important from the point of view of comfort, appearance and ease of maintenance. Patterns, prints, plaids and rough textures are less likely to show creases or stains, or bulges due to flesh, appliances, seating or sagging of the fabric.

The fashion for dressing in separates is the answer to many problems ranging from incontinence, where clothes below the waist may need far more frequent changes than those above, to atypical measurements—say, a size 14 top and a size 18 bottom. Two small garments are easier to handle and maintain than one larger one and are likely to be better for independent dressing. Waistcoats, of any length, will hide gaps between skirt or trousers and top, blending them into a harmonious outfit whilst concealing the silhouette.

Thoughtfully placed pockets can dispense with the need for a handbag, thus leaving the hands free.

Kaftans and smocks and many of today's leisure garments will conceal practically anything.

Trousers are acceptable wear for all occasions, in appropriate fabrics, as are skirts of any length; so if stockings and suspenders, or tights, have presented a problem in the past there is now no need whatsoever to wear them.

Specially designed clothing for the handicapped must be easy to put on and take off; larger armholes, wider cuffs, step-in dresses, button-through or wrap-around garments and pull-on clothes in stretch fabrics may all help to overcome difficulties. Back-fastening styles may be the most suitable for people who have to be dressed but who can sit up, provided that the fastening itself will not be uncomfortable in wear.

Fastenings must be easy to get at and to manipulate. Zips can be used decoratively. Sometimes seams can be opened up to insert fastenings—raglan, shoulder or princess-line seams, for example. *Velcro*, the touch-and-close fastener (used in small 'dabs' rather than in long strips which can be extremely difficult to place together accurately) snap-fasteners, poppers, hooks and eyes, easy-to-grasp buttons—the particular virtues of all these need to be considered for each case.

But at all times bear in mind the two elements of camouflage—concealment, by the use of colours and textures that do not attract attention, unconstricting and undemanding cut and styling together with patterned fabrics that blur exact outlines—and the use of a variety of tricks to attract the attention of both wearer and onlooker elsewhere, away from the handicap; these tricks might consist of features that shine, glitter or move, are particularly fashionable, beautiful or surprising, interesting detail or trimming, the contrast of plain and printed fabrics. Dull-surfaced, dark colours conceal, bright, brilliant colours attract. Use lines to give the illusion of increased length or width where it would be helpful. Nothing confuses the eye and conceals the exact outline of the figure so much as lines used diagonally. As well as checked or striped—or regularly patterned—fabrics that can be used on the bias there are those that are printed or woven so as to give a diagonal effect when they are used on the straight grain—thus achieving most of the optical advantage (but without the same quality of drape or cling as have most unsupported bias-cut garments) with none of the problems such as the sagging, the unwelcome clinging or the uneconomic cut.

94   Probably the first thing we notice about anybody's clothes is their **colour**—unless that happens to be merely dark or dull or neutral. Look around at the colour schemes people wear; the ones that are really good to look at are invariably those that compliment the natural colouring in some way, that are sympathetic to the skin tones and that also blend harmoniously with each other or contrast excitingly.

Collect a bagful of scraps of coloured fabrics, stir them around and see the effects they have on one another, lay them one by one on your own skin, separate, without looking, pairs of colours and then, no matter how dreary or dull they look together, hunt for another colour—or colours—that will react on both of them and turn them into an attractive, usable scheme. Colours can warm, cool, accentuate, stimulate, soften, flatter, contrast, tone with, enliven, sober down—or clash unpleasantly with each other. Their effects can be positive, negative, or merely neutral and it is up to the designer to seize every opportunity to create beautiful and appropriate effects.

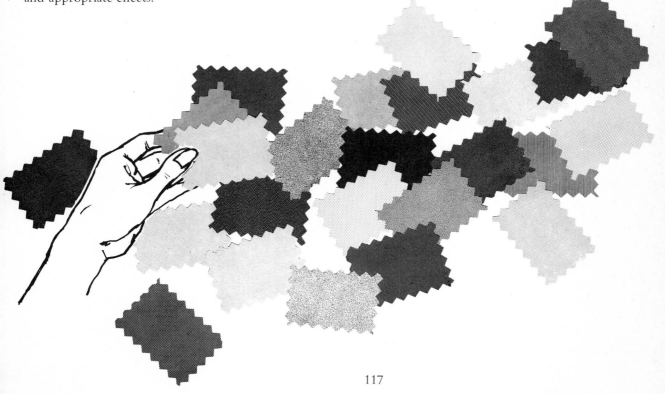

When designing for an individual select fabrics that enhance good colour features either by contrasting with or by complementing them; for instance, red hair can look marvellous worn with vivid blues or greens but even more exciting with the right shades of orange or red or tan or yellow; blue eyes look bluer still when blue is worn; black skins can look superb with browns and beiges, often really stunning with shades of purple and bottle green . . . Colours can be used to disguise less pleasing natural colouring; a red face will look hotter still in contrast with cool greens—certain shades of red would be a better choice; even better would be a multi-coloured tweed or print which contains some red, but it is impossible to know what will be best without the fabrics actually held against the face. Women with sallow skins are unlikely to look good in mauve; but always the rule is to *look* at the effects before coming to any decisions. Cream is often preferable to stark white which can show teeth and skin to disadvantage. Make-up, hair colouring, a sun tan—all these have their effects on the colours of clothes. Most people have their particular likes and prejudices; but colouring changes with age, fashions in colour introduce new combinations and ideas that it would be a pity to ignore. Some manufacturer's colour ranges are unbelievably crude and unsympathetic, having no relation whatsoever to any woman's natural colouring—man-made fibre fabrics more than natural ones tend to err in this direction.

95 **Textures** affect colours—shiny, rough, fluffy; again *look* at their effects. Blending colours together, softening the overall picture by the use of prints and tweeds and trimmings are tricks that can be used by the clever designer, alive to the need to create beautiful, helpful, appropriate and truly wearable clothes that relate to the woman underneath, her needs, her life-style and her environment today.

Index